A PRACTICAL SPANISH GRAMMAR

A PRACTICAL
SPANISH GRAMMAR

John G. Friar and George W. Kelly

Doubleday & Company, Inc.

Garden City, New York

Adapted from "A Practical Spanish Grammar for Border Patrol Officers" by the Immigration and Naturalization Service, U. S. Department of Justice.

PREFACE

The primary purpose of this course in Spanish is to furnish the minimum essentials of Spanish grammar in a very short period of time. The book has been purposely condensed in order to make its use practical.

The fundamentals of Spanish grammar are given in the lessons and the first part of the Appendix. Practice material follows.

The Spanish-English vocabulary includes only the Spanish words used in the text. The English-Spanish vocabulary includes many words that are not in the text, but that should be helpful. A rather complete list of idiomatic expressions has been given with particular attention to those used in Mexico. A very large list of words alike, or almost alike, in spelling, and alike in meaning in at least one acceptation is included in order to assist the advanced student in enlarging his vocabulary, and also, to show the great similarity of the two languages.

Acknowledgment is made of the valuable assistance given during the present revision of this work by Julio Ramírez, Jefe del Servicio de Población, Juárez, Chih., Mexico, and his staff.

CONTENTS

8

A PRACTICAL SPANISH GRAMMAR

THE ALPHABET

The Spanish alphabet consists of the same letters as the English alphabet and these four additional characters: CH, LL, Ñ, and RR.

A   Closely resembles "A" in "father."

alto—high	mayo—May
allá—there	allí—there
aquí—here	antes—before

B   The "B" and "V" are pronounced exactly alike in Spanish. At the beginning of a breath group; that is, after a pause in speech, or the beginning of a sentence, and after the letters "M" or "N" they are pronounced about like the "B" in book.

bonita—pretty	hombre—man
bajo—low	ambos—both
bien—well	hambre—hunger

At all other times the "B" and "V" are pronounced about like the "V" in "level."

hablar—to speak	libro—book
haber—to have	libra—pound
abril—April	libre—free

C   Soft like the "S" in "see" before "E" and "I." In Castilian Spanish the "C" before "E" and "I" and the "Z" in all instances are pronounced about like the "th" in "thin."

centavo—cent	cincuenta—fifty
cerca—near	cicatriz—scar
cinco—five	civil—civil

Hard like "C" in "country" at all other times.

caballo—horse	comer—to eat
calle—street	color—color
casa—house	cuando—when

CH   Like the "CH" in "church" at all times. This is the first of the Spanish characters that differ from the English. It is found in the dictionary immediately following the "C" and not as in English.

mucho—much	chico—child
muchacho—boy	choque—wreck
chiste—joke	marchar—to march

D   At the beginning of a breath group and after "L" and "N" it is pronounced about as it is in English with the tongue against the upper front teeth.

donde—where	indio—Indian
dar—to give	mandar—to order
el día—the day	el defecto—the defect

Following other letters about like the "TH" in "they."

madre—mother	cuidado—care
padre—father	ciudad[1]—city
lado—side	usted[1]—you

E   Has two sounds in Spanish. In open syllables (syllables in which it is the final letter) about like the English long "A"; but without the diphthongal sound often made in English.

leche—milk	enero—January
café—coffee, brown, café	leña—firewood

In closed syllables (one in which another letter follows) about like the English "E" in "bet."

ser—to be	el—the
estar—to be	en—in
comer—to eat	entrar—to enter

F   About as in English.

falta—fault	flor—flower
falsa—false	fe—faith
fecha—date	favor—favor

G   Before the vowels "A," "O," and "U" and all the consonants like the "G" in "go."

ganar—to earn	gustar—to be pleasing
gasolina—gasoline	guante—glove
gota—drop	grande—large
golpe—blow	gris—gray

Before "E" and "I" the "G" is pronounced like the "H" in "house."

gente—people	giro—draft
agente—agent	gigante—giant

[1] Many Spanish-speaking people fail to pronounce distinctly the final letter "D" of a word, saying rather "ciudá" and "usté."

In order to retain the "G" sound of "go" before "E" or "I," it is necessary to insert "U" after the "G," and the "U" is silent.

guía—guide   guerrero—warrior
guerra—war   Guillermo—William

If it is desired to retain the "U" sound following "G" before "E" or "I," place the dieresis (two dots) over the "U."

averigüé—I ascertained   vergüenza—shame

H   This letter is silent[2] in Spanish.

humano—human   hasta—until
hacer—to do   húmedo—humid
hermosa—beautiful   almohada—pillow
huelga—strike (work) huevo—egg
hueso—bone   huero—blond

I   Like the "I" in the English word "machine."

idea—idea   linda—pretty
idioma—language   comida—dinner
iglesia—church   isla—island

J   This letter is strongly aspirated like the "H" in the English word "house."

juez—judge   jueves—Thursday
Juan—John   jardín—garden
junio—June   mujer—woman
julio—July   reloj[3]—watch

K   This letter is found only in foreign words and is pronounced in the same manner as it is in the foreign word.

L   About as it is in English with the tongue nearly flat and the tip close to the front teeth.

lago—lake   leer—to read
lana—wool   lejos—far
lápiz—pencil   lugar—place

LL This is the second of the Spanish characters that differ from the English. It is considered as a single symbol and not as a double letter. It is found in the dictionary directly after the "L." In Mexico this letter is pronounced like the English consonant "Y." Castilian

---

[2] This letter is very slightly aspirated before the diphthong "UE"; however, in many instances the aspiration is so slight that it is almost imperceptible.

[3] Many Spanish-speaking persons pronounce this word "reló," and in some instances it will be found so written.

Spanish calls for the sound of the "LLI" of "million." It is well to learn to use and to distinguish both.

ella—she	llegar—to arrive
llave—key	lluvia—rain
llevar—to carry	llegada—arrival

M As in English.

mapa—map	más—more
María—Mary	mes—month
martes—Tuesday	manera—manner

N As in English.

nada—nothing	nombre—name
nadie—nobody	noche—night
nunca—never	anoche—last night

Ñ This is the third of the Spanish characters that differ from the English, and it is found after the "N" in the dictionary. It has the value of the "NY" of "canyon."

montaña—mountain	compañía—company
niño—child (boy)	albañil—mason
leña—firewood	mañana—tomorrow

O In open syllables like the "O" in "obey."

ocho—eight	oro—gold
oficina—office	permiso—permission
ojo—eye	recibo—receipt

In closed syllables like the "O" in "order."

son—they are	con—with
señor—sir	sombrero—hat
vapor—ship	por—by, through

P About as in English.

peso—dollar, peso	puerto—port
pagar—to pay	para—in order to
puerta—door	pelo—hair

Q This letter is always followed by "U" and in turn by either "E" or "I," and the "U" is always silent. The "QU" has the value of the English "K."

querer—to wish	quien—who
quince—fifteen	quebrar—to break
¿qué?—what?	quemar—to burn

R This letter is slightly trilled in Spanish. At the beginning of a word it is very strongly trilled.

pero—but	razón—reason
sobre—on	renta—rent
primero—first	tener—to have
parte—part	venir—to come

RR This is the last of the Spanish characters that differ from the English letters. It is found after the letter "R" in the dictionary. It is very strongly trilled.

perro—male dog	carro—car
perra—female dog	herrero—blacksmith
hierro—iron	cigarro—cigarette

S About like the "S" in the English word "sister."

bastante—enough	contestar—to answer
buscar—to seek	cosa—thing
casa—house	bosque—forest

The "S" preceding "D" or "M" has a buzzing sound.

desde—from, since	mismo—same

T As in English.

tarde—late	triste—sad
tez—complexion	turista—tourist
taza—cup	también—also

U As a vowel like the "OO" of "moon."

último—last	único—only
un—one or a	luna—moon
usar—to use	sujeto—subject

For "U" as a consonant, see diphthongs.

V See "B."

voy—I am going	evidencia—evidence
viaje—trip	tuve—I had
invierno—winter	jueves—Thursday
enviar—to send	curva—curve

W This letter appears only in foreign words and is pronounced as it is in the foreign word in which it appears.

X This letter has the value of the English "GS" between vowels.

exacto—exact	examinar—to examine
exactamente—exactly	examen—examination

It is pronounced like the English "S" before consonants. Some people pronounce the "X" before a consonant in Spanish as it is pronounced in English.

explicar—to explain
extranjero—foreigner

extensión—extension
expreso—express

Y Standing alone it means "and" and is pronounced like the English long "E."

As a consonant it is pronounced like the "Y" in "Yuma."

yo—I
ya—already

yerno—son-in-law
leyó—he read

See diphthongs for its use in diphthongs.

Z Has the same value as "C" before "E" or "I."

zapato—shoe
zapatero—shoemaker
zapatería—shoeshop

comenzar—to begin
empezar—to begin
vez—time (numerically)

This letter rarely appears before "E" or "I" in Spanish. In conjugating verbs the "Z" is changed to "C" before "E." There are no conjugations where the letter "I" follows "Z."

DIPHTHONGS

Diphthongs in Spanish are formed by the following combinations of vowels in one syllable: a weak plus a strong vowel, a strong plus a weak vowel, or two weak vowels. The strong vowels are "A," "E," and "O"; the weak ones are "I," "U," and "Y." Two strong vowels cannot appear in the same syllable. In order to retain the full value of a weak vowel when it appears in combination with a strong vowel, it is necessary to place the written accent over the weak vowel. This results in two syllables and breaks up the diphthong.

AI or **AY** About like the "Y" in "rye."

aire—air
hay—there is (are)

traigo—I bring
tráigame—bring me

EI or **EY** About like the "EY" in "they."

rey—king
reina—queen

seis—six
veinte—twenty

OI or **OY** About like the "OY" in "boy."

doy—I give
voy—I am going
oigo—I hear

soy—I am
hoy—today
estoy—I am

AU About like the "OW" in "cow."

cautivo—captive
autor—author

aunque—although
causa—cause

EU   An "E" plus "U" sound as in

Europa—Europe   **reumatismo**—rheumatism

OU   Very rare.

In the following groups the "U" and "I" preceding other vowels are often considered as semiconsonants and have the value of "W" and "Y" respectively.

UA

¿**cuánto?**—how much?   **cuatro**—four
¿**cuándo?**—when?   **cuarto**—fourth, room

UE

puerta—door   **nuevo**—new
puente—bridge   **cuerpo**—body

UO

cuota—quota or share

IA

hacia—toward   **farmacia**—pharmacy
estudia—he studies   **Alemania**—Germany

IE

pierna—leg   **tiempo**—time
diente—tooth   **viejo**—old

IO

adiós—goodbye   **precio**—price
palacio—palace   **recibió**—he received

IU

triunfo—triumph   **ciudadano**—citizen
ciudad—city   **ciudadanía**—citizenship

UI

cuidado—care   **ruido**—noise

In all of the foregoing diphthongs the stress of the voice falls on the strong vowel when the syllable is stressed. In the case of two weak vowels the stress is on the second of the two when the syllable is stressed.

"UE" or "UI" following "Q" or "G" are not diphthongs, the "U" being silent.

SYLLABICATION

In dividing words into syllables the following principles should be observed:

A consonant goes with the following vowel.

a-mi-go   e-ne-ro   ma-ña-na

Two strong vowels are separated.

le-o   ca-er   lí-ne-a   le-e

Two consonants coming between vowels are usually separated.

cin-co   pron-to   her-ma-no   par-te

The letters "CH," "LL," and "RR" are considered as one letter and are never separated.

mu-cha-cho   ca-lle   ci-ga-rro   pe-rro

A consonant followed by "R" or "L" is not separated from the "R" or "L" except "RL," "SL," "TL," "SR," and "NR."

ha-blar   li-bro   en-trar   hom-bre

but:

is-la   per-la   at-las   char-la

The letters of a diphthong or triphthong are not separated.

jui-cio   puer-ta   a-pre-ciáis   hue-ro

If the weak vowel of a diphthong or triphthong is accented, or the first vowel when both are weak, the accent mark is placed over said vowel to show that there is no longer a diphthong or triphthong.

dí-a   le-í-do   flú-i-do   da-rí-ais

The last of more than two consonants coming between vowels goes with the following vowel.

cons-tan-te   pers-pec-ti-va   ins-tan-te

A prefix forms a separate syllable.

ex-pre-sar   des-a-gra-da-ble

ACCENTUATION

Words ending in a vowel or "N" or "S" receive the stress of the voice regularly on the next to the last syllable. In the following list the words are divided into syllables, and the syllable receiving the stress is underlined.

ju lio—July
a mi go—friend
fe cha—date

u na—one, a
tra ba jo—work
di ne ro—money

Words ending in a consonant other than "N" or "S" receive the stress of the voice regularly on the last syllable.

ve nir—to come
mu jer—woman
pa pel—paper

ca lor—heat
co lor—color
de se ar—to desire

Words stressed contrary to the two foregoing rules bear the written accent over the vowel of the syllable to be stressed.

lec ción—lesson
fá cil—easy
di fí cil—difficult

ár bo les—trees
a quí—here
jó ve nes—youths

Certain words bear the written accent in order to distinguish them from other words otherwise spelled alike and pronounced alike, but having an entirely different meaning.

él—he	el—the	sólo—only	solo—alone
sí—yes	si—if	más—more	mas—but
mí—me	mi—my	dé—give	de—of, from
tú—you	tu—your	té—tea	te—you

The written accent is used to distinguish the interrogative or exclamatory from the relative use of pronouns and adverbs.

¿cuánto?—how much?	¿cómo?—how?	¿cuál?—which?
cuanto—as much	como—like	cual—which
¿cuándo?—when?	¿qué?—what?	¿quién?—who?
cuando—when	que—that	quien—who

The written accent over the weak vowel of a weak plus strong or strong plus weak combination breaks up the diphthong and results in two separate syllables.

creído—(believed)	is a three syllable word	cre í do
leído—(read)	is a three syllable word	le í do
leímos—(we read)	is a three syllable word	le í mos
país—(country)	is a two syllable word	pa ís

PUNCTUATION

Punctuation is the same in Spanish as in English with the following exceptions:

A question has an inverted question mark (¿) at the beginning of the question as well as the regular question mark (?) at the end.

¿(En) Dónde está Juan?	Where is John?
¿Cómo está Vd.?	How are you?

An exclamation has the inverted exclamation mark (¡) at the beginning of the interjection as well as the regular exclamation mark (!) at the end.

¡Qué bonita!	How pretty!
¡Qué lástima!	What a pity!

In quotations a dash (—) is generally used to indicate a change of speaker instead of quotation marks.

Juan dijo:—Yo no voy. —Ni yo tampoco.—Respondió Ana.
John said: "I am not going." "Nor I either," responded Anna.

The days of the week and the months of the year are not capitalized unless at the beginning of a sentence.

Hoy es lunes.	Today is Monday.
Es el dos de mayo.	It is the second of May.

The pronoun "yo" (I) is not capitalized, except at the beginning of a sentence.

An adjective of nationality is not capitalized. Some authors capitalize adjectives of nationality used as nouns while others do not.

Yo hablo español.	I speak Spanish.
Hablo a un francés. ⎫	I am speaking to
Hablo a un Francés. ⎬	a Frenchman.

The following abbreviations are capitalized:

usted	Vd.	señor	Sr.
ustedes	Vds.	señora	Sra.
	señorita	Srta.	

LESSON II

THE PARTS OF SPEECH

There are eight parts of speech in Spanish as well as in English: nouns, pronouns, adjectives (the articles will be treated as adjectives), verbs, adverbs, prepositions, conjunctions, and interjections.

NOUNS

A noun is the name of a person, place, or thing. A proper noun is the name of a particular person, place, or thing.

John—**Juan**	Mary—**María**
Charles—**Carlos**	Anna—**Ana**
Henry—**Enrique**	Louise—**Luisa**
Paul—**Pablo**	El Paso—**El Paso**
Mexico—**México**	Texas—**Tejas**

The Imperial Hotel—**El Hotel Imperial**

A common noun is a common name for persons, places, or things that are of the same class or kind.

boy—**muchacho**	town—**pueblo**
year—**año**	book—**libro**
week—**semana, ocho días**	passport—**pasaporte**
river—**río**	month—**mes**
visa—**visa**	bridge—**puente**

In English there are three genders: masculine, feminine, and neuter. In Spanish all nouns are masculine or feminine, there being no neuter. Generally nouns ending in "O" are masculine, and nouns ending in "A" are feminine. Names of male beings are masculine, and names of female beings are feminine. All nouns should be learned with the definite article. (See Articles under Adjectives.)

the boy—**el niño**	the brother—**el hermano**
the girl—**la niña**	the sister—**la hermana**
the state—**el estado**	the money—**el dinero**
the pen—**la pluma**	the silver—**la plata**
the gold—**el oro**	the silver—**el dinero**

There are several exceptions to the above, such as:

the hand—**la mano**   the map—**el mapa**   the day—**el día**

25

Nouns not ending in "O" or "A" should be memorized with the definite article.

the paper—**el papel**	the age—**la edad**
the city—**la ciudad**	the foot—**el pie**
the woman—**la mujer**	the man—**el hombre**

Nouns ending in a vowel form their plurals by adding "S," and those ending in a consonant form their plurals by adding "ES." Those ending in "Z" change the "Z" to "C" before adding "ES."

the son—**el hijo**	the sons—**los hijos**
the daughter—**la hija**	the daughters—**las hijas**
the woman—**la mujer**	the women—**las mujeres**
the pencil—**el lápiz**	the pencils—**los lápices**

PRONOUNS

A pronoun is a word that takes the place of, or is used instead of, a noun. Listed below are the English and Spanish subject pronouns with the persons and numbers:

Subject Pronouns

1st.	I	(yo)	person speaking	we	(nosotros, as)	1st.
2nd.	you	(tú)	person spoken to	you	(vosotros, as)	2nd.
3rd.	he	(él)	person spoken of	they	(ellos, masc.)	3rd.
3rd.	she	(ella)	person spoken of	they	(ellas, fem.)	3rd.
3rd.	you	(Vd.)	person spoken of	you	(Vds.)	3rd.

In Spanish there are two ways of saying "you," each having a singular and a plural form as listed above. "Tú" and its plural "vosotros, as" are called the familiar form and are used in speaking to members of one's family, intimate friends, servants, and animals. This form is the true second person and is used with the second person form of the verb. "Vd." and its plural "Vds." are called the formal or polite form. These are abbreviations of "usted" and "ustedes" respectively. In writing they may be written in the abbreviated form or written completely. This form is derived from "vuestra merced" and "vuestras mercedes" meaning "your grace." This form is used only with the third person of the verb.

ADJECTIVES

An adjective is a word that modifies (limits or describes) a noun or a pronoun.

alto—tall	**diez**—ten
bonito—pretty	**pocos**—few
nuevo—new	**viejo**—old

azul—blue
mucho—much

muchos—many
tres—three

Adjectives agree with the noun or pronoun that they modify in gender and number.

Adjectives form their plural in the same manner as do nouns. (See Nouns.)

Adjectives ending in "O" in the masculine change the "O" to "A" to form the feminine. Other adjectives are the same for both genders. Exception: Adjectives of nationality ending in a consonant in the masculine singular add "A" to form the feminine.

Masculine				Feminine	
Singular	Plural			Singular	Plural
blanco	blancos	(white)		blanca	blancas
alto	altos	(tall)		alta	altas
grande	grandes	(large)		grande	grandes
español	españoles	(Spanish)		española	españolas
inglés	ingleses	(English)		inglesa	inglesas
mexicano	mexicanos	(Mexican)		mexicana	mexicanas

Limiting adjectives precede the noun they modify; descriptive adjectives generally follow the noun they modify.

muchos libros	many books
muchos libro rojos	many red books
nuestra casa	our house
nuestra casa grande	our large house
diez caballos	ten horses
diez caballos negros	ten black horses

ARTICLES

The definite and indefinite articles in Spanish are adjectives and precede the noun and agree with it in number and gender.

Definite				Indefinite	
Masculine		Feminine		Masculine	Feminine
Sing.	el	la		un	una
Plu.	los	las		no plurals[4]	

el muchacho alto	the tall boy
los muchachos altos	the tall boys
la pluma verde	the green pen
las plumas verdes	the green pens
un libro rojo	a red book
una muchacha bonita	a pretty girl

[4] This does not apply to "unos" and "unas," which have the form of the plural articles but mean "some."

27

VERBS

A verb is a word that shows action, being, or state of being.

John <u>writes</u> a letter.	"action"
John <u>is</u> a boy.	"being"
John <u>is</u> sick.	"state of being"

comprar—to buy	**vender**—to sell
estar—to be	**comer**—to eat
entrar—to enter	**ser**—to be
decir—to tell	**escribir**—to write
recibir—to receive	**pasar**—to pass

ADVERBS

An adverb is a word that modifies a verb, an adjective, or another adverb.

cerca—near	**claramente**—clearly	**aquí**—here
lejos—far	**fácilmente**—easily	**allí**—there
muy—very	**más**—more	**bien**—well

Él habla claramente.	He speaks clearly.	(Modifying a verb)
Ella es muy bonita.	She is very pretty.	(Modifying an adjective)
Él habla muy bien.	He speaks very well.	(Modifying an adverb)

PREPOSITIONS

A preposition is a word that shows the relation of a noun or pronoun following it to some other word in the sentence.

de—from, of	**sobre**—on, upon	**con**—with
desde—from	**por**—by, through, for	**en**—on, in
a—at, to	**para**—for, in order to	**sin**—without

El libro está <u>en</u> la mesa.	The book is <u>on</u> the table.
Yo escribo <u>con</u> pluma y tinta.	I write <u>with</u> pen and ink.
La silla es <u>para</u> Vd.	The chair is <u>for</u> you.

CONJUNCTIONS

A conjunction is a word that is used to join a word or group of words to a word or to a group of words.

y—and	**porque**—because	**pero**—but
si—if	**aunque**—although	**o**—or

El lápiz <u>y</u> la pluma están aquí.	The pencil <u>and</u> pen are here.
Tengo cinco <u>o</u> seis pesos.	I have five <u>or</u> six pesos (dollars).

28

INTERJECTIONS

An interjection is a word that expresses strong or sudden feeling.

¡Qué lástima!—What a pity!   ¡Qué bonita!—How pretty!

THE SENTENCE

A sentence is a group of words expressing a complete thought. It has two parts, the subject (noun or pronoun) and its modifiers, and the predicate (verb) and its modifiers.

The subject is that part about which something is said, and the predicate tells that which is said about the subject. The subject is broken up into the subject word and it modifiers, and the predicate is broken up into the predicate word and its modifiers.

The black horse / ran a beautiful race. "The black horse" is the complete subject, "horse" being the subject word modified by the adjectives "the" and "black." "Ran a beautiful race" is the complete predicate, "ran" being the predicate word modified by the phrase "a beautiful race."

THE PRESENT INDICATIVE TENSE

In Spanish, verbs are conjugated to show mood, tense, person, and number. Most verbs are conjugated after a regular pattern. Verbs that do not follow the pattern are said to be irregular and must be committed to memory. Even these irregular verbs are not irregular in all tenses. (See page 139.)

The present indicative tense in Spanish means that the time spoken of is present and indicates or points out a thing as material or existing. It may be used to make a statement or to ask a question, either affirmatively or negatively.

> 1st conjugation, **habl-AR**—to speak
> 2nd conjugation, **vend-ER**—to sell
> 3rd conjugation, **viv-IR**—to live

The infinitive is the key word that is used to form all conjugations and tenses. The present indicative tense is formed by dropping the infinitive endings "AR," "ER," and "IR," and to the remainder, which is the stem, attaching the proper endings. From the infinitive of all regular "AR" verbs, of which **hablar** is an example, the "AR" ending is dropped, and to the remainder "habl," which is the stem, are attached the following endings: o, as, a, amos, áis, an.

yo	hablo	1st person singular	The person speaking	I
tú	hablas	2nd person singular	The person spoken to	you
él	habla	3rd person singular	The person spoken of	he
ella	habla	3rd person singular	The person spoken of	she
Vd.	habla	3rd person singular	The person spoken of	you
nosotros, as	hablamos	1st p. pl.	The persons speaking	we
vosotros, as	habláis	2nd p. pl.	The persons spoken to	you
ellos	hablan	3rd p. pl.	The persons spoken of	they
ellas	hablan	3rd p. pl.	The persons spoken of	they
Vds.	hablan	3rd p. pl.	The persons spoken of	you

From the infinitive of all regular "ER" verbs, of which **vender** is an example, the "ER" ending is dropped and to the remainder, "vend," which is the stem, are attached the following endings: o, es, e, emos, éis, en.

yo	vendo	nosotros, as	vendemos
tú	vendes	vosotros, as	vendéis
él	vende	ellos	venden
ella	vende	ellas	venden
Vd.	vende	Vds.	venden

From the infinitive of all regular "IR" verbs, of which **vivir** is an example, the "IR" ending is dropped and to the remainder, "viv," which is the stem, are attached the following ending: o, es, e, imos, ís, en.

yo	vivo	nosotros, as	vivimos
tú	vives	vosotros, as	vivís
él	vive	ellos	viven
ella	vive	ellas	viven
Vd.	vive	Vds.	viven

The present indicative of these verbs translates in the following ways in English:

Yo hablo.	I speak. I do speak. I am speaking.
¿Hablo yo?	Do I speak? Am I speaking?
Yo no hablo.	I do not speak. I am not speaking.
¿No hablo yo?	Do I not speak? Am I not speaking?
Tú hablas.	You speak. You do speak. You are speaking.
¿Hablas tú?	Do you speak? Are you speaking?
Tú no hablas.	You do not speak. You are not speaking.
¿No hablas tú?	Do you not speak? Are you not speaking?
Él habla.	He speaks. He does speak. He is speaking.
¿Habla él?	Does he speak? Is he speaking?
Él no habla.	He does not speak. He is not speaking.
¿No habla él?	Does he not speak? Is he not speaking?
Ella habla.	She speaks. She does speak. She is speaking.
¿Habla ella?	Does she speak? Is she speaking?
Ella no habla.	She does not speak. She is not speaking.
¿No habla ella?	Does she not speak? Is she not speaking?
Vd. habla.	You speak. You do speak. You are speaking.
¿Habla Vd.?	Do you speak? Are you speaking?
Vd. no habla.	You do not speak. You are not speaking.
¿No habla Vd.?	Do you not speak? Are you not speaking?

The plural forms are used in the same manner as above. Notice that the negative **"no"** immediately precedes the verb.

Following are a few regular verbs that are conjugated in the present indicative tense by following the key given on pages 30 and 31.

AR	
comprar—to buy	pesar—to weigh
pagar—to pay	ganar—to earn
usar—to use	dudar—to doubt
entrar—to enter	cortar—to cut
	gastar—to spend

AR	
pasar—to pass	ayudar—to help
llamar—to call	llegar—to arrive
sacar—to take out	terminar—to finish
desear—to desire	trabajar—to work
tomar—to take	
tomar—to drink	**ER**
aconsejar—to advise	aprender—to learn
arrestar—to arrest	comer—to eat
deportar—to deport	beber—to drink
estudiar—to study	vender—to sell
olvidar—to forget	deber—to owe
llevar—to carry	
acabar—to finish	**IR**
esperar—to hope	escribir—to write
esperar—to wait for	vivir—to live
solicitar—to solicit	recibir—to receive
contestar—to answer	residir—to reside
	abrir—to open

WORD ORDER IN SPANISH SENTENCES

In general, the word order of Spanish sentences is the same as in English. In a question the subject usually follows the verb. The auxiliary verb "do" is not translated from English to Spanish. Examples:

English sentence	Spanish word order	Spanish translation
Do you speak to John?	Speak you to John?	¿Habla Vd. a Juan?
Do you eat here?	Eat you here?	¿Come Vd. aquí?
Do you have any money?	Have you money?	¿Tiene Vd. dinero?

The same is true of the auxiliary (helping) verb "to be" except when used to form the passive voice or the progressive tenses.

English sentence	Spanish word order	Spanish translation
Are you going to town?	Go you to the town?	¿Va Vd. al pueblo?
Where is Mary living?	Where lives Mary?	¿Dónde vive María?

CONTRACTIONS

In Spanish the masculine singular definite article "el" contracts with the prepositions "a" and "de" respectively.

"a" plus "el" equals "al"—to the, at the
"de" plus "el" equals "del"—of the, from the

This contraction does not occur with the feminine definite articles "la" or "las" nor with the masculine plural definite article "los." The word "él" meaning "he" does not contract with the above prepositions.

POSSESSION OF NOUNS

The possession of nouns corresponding to the English " 's" or "s' " (apostrophe s, or s apostrophe) is expressed in Spanish by the use of the preposition "de" placed before the possessor.

The girl's book.	The book of the girl.	El libro de la niña.
Mary's pencils.	The pencils of Mary.	Los lápices de María.
The boys' home.	The home of the boys.	La casa de los niños.

USE OF PREPOSITION "OF" TO REPLACE ADJECTIVAL NOUNS

In Spanish a noun is never used as an adjective to show the material of which a thing is made as in English. Instead, the object and material of which it is constructed are joined by the preposition "de."

English	Spanish word order	Spanish translation
the straw hat	the hat of straw	el sombrero de paja
the silk shirt	the shirt of silk	la camisa de seda
the wool suit	the suit of wool	el traje de lana

VOCABULARY

la casa—the house
el muchacho—the boy
la muchacha—the girl

el libro—the book
la pluma—the pen
el lápiz—the pencil

la tinta—the ink
la silla—the chair
hablar—to speak
aprender—to learn
vivir—to live
con—with
de—of, from
en—in, on
a—to, at
la lección—the lesson
el sombrero—the hat
el niño—the child (m)

la niña—the child (f)
la mesa—the table
el cuarto—the room
María—Mary
Juan—John
Tejas—Texas
comprar—to buy
vender—to sell
escribir—to write
aquí—here
y—and
la clase—the class

EXERCISE

1. El muchacho compra un lápiz. 2. Ella escribe la lección. 3. Nosotros vivimos en El Paso. 4. Juan escribe con pluma y tinta. 5. Vd. compra una mesa y un sombrero. 6. El niño de María vive en Arizona. 7. Yo vivo aquí. 8. Juan vive en California. 9. Ellos venden el sombrero a la muchacha. 10. Él y yo vivimos[5] en Tucsón. 11. La muchacha vive en Tejas. 12. El muchacho vive con Juan. 13. Ellos aprenden la lección. 14. Yo vendo el sombrero del muchacho. 15. Ella escribe con un lápiz.

EXERCISE

1. He writes the lesson. 2. She buys a table and a chair. 3. John learns the lesson. 4. I sell the boy's hat. 5. The boy and the girl live here. 6. I write with Mary's pencil. 7. We write with pen and ink. 8. The children live here. 9. John sells the children's books. 10. We buy the boys' hats. 11. John and Mary do not live here. 12. They write with pen and ink. 13. He is learning the lesson. 14. I live with John. 15. We write with the boy's pencil.

[5] When the first person is used with any other person, the Spanish verb will be in the first person plural.

"TENER" AND "HABER"

The verbs **"tener"** and **"haber,"** both meaning "to have," are irregular in the present indicative tense.

Tener		Haber	
tengo	tenemos	he	hemos
tienes	tenéis	has	habéis
tiene	tienen	ha	han

"Tener" means "to have" showing possession and is not to be used interchangeably with **"haber,"** which means "to have" as an auxiliary verb in forming the compound tenses.

The past participle of regular verbs is formed by adding "ado" to the stem of verbs of the first conjugation and "ido" to the stem of verbs of the second and third conjugations.

tomar—tom ado
comer—com ido
vivir—viv ido

The present perfect indicative tense (called "perfect" by many grammarians) is formed by placing the present tense of the auxiliary verb **"haber"** immediately in front of the past participle of the main verb.

Tomar	Comer	Vivir
he tomado	he comido	he vivido
has tomado	has comido	has vivido
ha tomado	ha comido	ha vivido
hemos tomado	hemos comido	hemos vivido
habéis tomado	habéis comido	habéis vivido
han tomado	han comido	han vivido

No word can come between the auxiliary verb and the past participle.

Él ha comido.	He has eaten.
¿Ha comido Vd.?	Have you eaten?
Yo no he comido.	I have not eaten.

VOCABULARY

el amigo—the friend (m)	el dinero—the money
la amiga—the friend (f)	el papá—the papa

el padre—the father	bueno—good
la madre—the mother	¿hay?—is there? are there?
la mamá—the mama	malo—bad
la calle—the street	mucho—much, a great deal
el hijo—the son	muchos—many
la hija—the daughter	poco—little (amount)
el hombre—the man	pocos—a few
la mujer—the woman	pequeño—small (size)
la carta—the letter	estudiar—to study
sí—yes	entrar (en)—to enter
¿qué?—what?	comer—to eat
hay—there is, there are	no—no

EXERCISE

1. Él no tiene mucho dinero. 2. ¿Qué vende Vd.? 3. Hay tres sillas en el cuarto. 4. (Yo) He estudiado las lecciones. 5. ¿Qué ha comido María? 6. Juan no tiene padre. 7. (Yo) Tengo un sombrero en la mesa. 8. María ha comprado una silla. 9. El amigo del hombre vende muchas sillas. 10. El muchacho no estudia mucho. 11. ¿Estudia Vd. mucho? 12. Hay un libro en la mesa. 13. Yo he tomado el libro del hombre. 14. La mujer ha vendido una casa. 15. Hay muchas cartas en la mesa de María. 15. Yo no vivo aquí.

EXERCISE

1. I do not have (any[6]) children. 2. There is much money on the table. 3. Charles has sold a good hat. 4. Is there a letter on the table? 5. I have bought a blue pencil. 6. How much money do you have? 7. Have you studied the lesson? 8. Have you bought many books? 9. The girl's mother has not eaten. 10. Does the boy's father eat here? 11. He does not speak much. 12. There are many boys in the room. 13. He has taken the money to the man. 14. We do not have many pens. 15. On what street do you live?

[6] The word "any" is generally omitted unless used for emphasis.

LESSON VI

"SER" AND "ESTAR"

The verbs **"ser"** and **"estar,"** both meaning "to be," are irregular in the present indicative tense. These verbs are never used interchangeably.

Ser		Estar	
soy	somos	estoy	estamos
eres	sois	estás	estáis
es	son	está	están

Estar is used:

To show location or position (place where a person or thing is, temporarily or permanently).

El libro está en la mesa.	The book is on the table.
Juárez está en México.	Juarez is in Mexico.
¿En dónde está Juan?	Where is John?

To express a condition that is accidental or temporary.

La mujer está enferma.	The woman is ill.
El agua está fría.	The water is cold.
La niña está pálida.	The girl is pale. (Now.)

With a past participle to express a resultant state. The past participle is used as an adjective and as such, agrees in gender and number with the subject of the sentence.

El libro está bien escrito.	The book is well written.
La mujer está sentada.	The woman is seated.
La puerta está cerrada.	The door is closed.

With a present participle to express progressive action (explained later).

Ser is used at all other times. Generally **"ser"** expresses a state or condition that is natural or inherent and essentially lasting rather than accidental or occasional. Such conditions may show: age, character, financial status, appearance, origin, ownership, material of which a thing is made, occupation, nationality, time expressions, impersonal expressions. It is **always** used before a predicate noun or pronoun.

Él es viejo.	He is old. (age)
Ella es buena.	She is good. (character)
El hombre es rico.	The man is rich. (financial)
Ellas son bonitas.	They are pretty. (appearance)
Yo soy de México.	I am from Mexico. (origin)
El libro es de Juan.	The book is John's. (possession)
El anillo es de oro.	The ring is gold. (material)
Él es médico.[7]	He is a doctor. (occupation)
Él es un buen médico.	He is a good doctor. (occupation)
Hoy es lunes.	Today is Monday. (time)
Ellos son mexicanos.	They are Mexicans. (nationality)
Son las dos y media.	It is two-thirty. (time)
¿De qué color es el libro?	What color is the book? (appearance)
Es imposible hacerlo.	It is impossible to do it. (impersonal expression)
Es él.	It is he. (predicate pronoun)

VOCABULARY

grande—large	el pasaporte—the passport
pequeño—small	la mano—the hand
viejo—old	Carlos—Charles
joven—young	el [9]agua—the water
nuevo—new	el lunar—the mole (mark)
rico—rich	la cicatriz—the scar
pobre—poor	el, la puente—the bridge
bonita—pretty	español—Spanish
frío—cold	inglés—English
caliente—hot, warm	el oro—the gold
el médico—the doctor	la plata—the silver
el anillo—the ring	¿dónde?—where?
la puerta—the door	donde—where (adverb)
el puerto—the port	mucho—much, a great deal (adv.)
México[8]—Mexico	poco—little, a little (adverb)
mexicano[8]—Mexican	pero—but
señor—sir, Mr.	cansado—tired
señora—madam, Mrs.	pasar—to pass, cross, spend time
señorita—Miss, young lady	beber—to drink
la escuela—the school	tomar—to take, drink
hoy—today	sacar—to take out

EXERCISE

1. El muchacho está en México. 2. Los libros son nuevos. 3. María es muy bonita. 4. Juan es un muchacho bueno. 5. Ellos están malos.

[7] The indefinite article is omitted before an unmodified predicate noun.

[8] The words "Mexico" and "Mexican" are written with an "x" or a "j." The use of the "x" prevails along the Mexican border and is official in Mexico.

[9] Feminine words beginning with a stressed "a" or "ha" take the masculine article in the singular for the sake of euphony.

6. Ella es muy rica. 7. ¿Dónde está el padre de Juan? 8. Él es mexicano. 9. ¿Dónde está el médico? 10. La señorita Brown[10] no es muy bonita. 11. El muchacho es el hijo de la señora. 12. ¿Dónde está el pasaporte de Carlos? 13. El agua está caliente. 14. El padre de la señorita no está aquí. 15. Él no estudia mucho. 16. La mujer está cansada. 17. La señora Brown no está en la escuela. 18. Juan es médico. 19. Ellos estudian poco y aprenden poco. 20. Nosotros somos grandes pero usted es pequeño.

EXERCISE

1. Where is the man's passport? 2. The gold ring is not here. 3. He is from Mexico. 4. Mary is very pretty. 5. The young lady is sick today. 6. The woman's son is in Denver. 7. The scar is not very large. 8. Is your mother sick today? 9. The ink is on the table. 10. The child is not here. 11. The lady's hat is not on the table. 12. He writes the lessons with pen and ink. 13. The young lady is not here. 14. The pencil is not red. 15. There is a chair in the room. 16. Miss Smith is not very tall. 17. Mr. Brown is a good doctor. 18. She is rich, but she is not well. 19. We are tired, but we are not sick. 20. The room is large.

[10] A proper name modified by a title requires the definite article immediately before the title except in direct address.

La señorita Smith está mala.	Miss Smith is sick.
El señor García come aquí.	Mr. Garcia eats here.
But: Buenos días, señor Brown.	Good morning, Mr. Brown.

PREPOSITIONAL PRONOUNS

The prepositional pronouns are the same as the subject pronouns with the exception of the first and second persons singular.

Singular	Plural
mí—me	nosotros, as—us
ti—you	vosotros, as—you
él—him	ellos—them
ella—her	ellas—them
Vd.—you	Vds.—you

When used after the preposition **"con,"** the first and second persons singular become **"conmigo"** (with me) and **"contigo"** (with you) respectively.

Este libro es para Vd.	This book is for you.
Ella no estudia conmigo.	She does not study with me.
María no viene con él.	Mary is not coming with him.
¿Estudia Juan contigo?	Does John study with you?

THE POLITE COMMAND OF REGULAR VERBS

The polite command is obtained from the third persons singular and plural of the present subjunctive with **"Vd."** and **"Vds."** respectively used as the subject of the command. It is obtained by adding the following endings to the stem of the verb:

"AR" VERBS	"ER" AND "IR" VERBS
e	a
en	an

Note that these endings are the reverse of the present indicative endings. Should the verb be irregular in the stem of the first person singular of the present indicative, that stem will be used to attach the command endings. There are three exceptions to this: See pages 76 and 103.

Aprenda Vd. su lección.	You (s) learn your lesson.
Aprendan Vds. su lección.	You (p) learn your lesson.
Escriba Vd. la carta.	You (s) write the letter.

Escriban Vds. las cartas.	You (p) write the letters.
Tome Vd. el libro.	You (s) take the book.
Tomen Vds. los libros.	You (p) take the books.

PRESENT INDICATIVE TENSE OF "DAR" AND "IR"

Dar (to give)		Ir (to go)	
doy	damos	voy	vamos
das	dais	vas	vais
da	dan	va	van

INTERROGATIVES—"¿QUÉ?," "¿CUÁL(ES)?," AND "¿QUIÉN(ES)?"

"¿Cuál(es)?" meaning "which?" refers to persons or things, and is used to select or choose one or more than one from a larger group.

¿Cuál de los libros es el suyo?	Which (one) of the books is yours?
¿Cuáles de los libros son los suyos?	Which (ones) of the books are yours?

"¿Cuál?" meaning "what?" is used before "ser," except when a definition is asked for in which case "¿qué?" is used.

¿Cuál es la fecha (de hoy)?	What is the date?
¿Cuál es su ocupación?	What is your occupation?
¿Cuál es su nacionalidad?	What is your nationality?
¿Qué es gramática?	What is grammar?
¿Qué es esto?	What is this?
¿Qué tiene Vd. en la mano?	What do you have in your hand?

At all other times, except in idioms, the English interrogative "what?" is rendered by "¿qué?" in Spanish.

¿Qué come Vd.?	What are you eating?
¿Qué estudia María?	What is Mary studying?
¿Qué escribe su mamá?	What does your mother write?

The interrogative "¿quién?" meaning "who?" or "whom?" refers to persons only.

¿Quién estudia con Juan?	Who is studying with John?
¿Con quién vive Vd.?	With whom do you live?
¿Quién tiene mi libro?	Who has my book?

VOCABULARY

enfermo—sick	el carro—the car
largo—long	la cosa—the thing
el alumno—the pupil	la familia—the family
el río—the river	el esposo—the husband

la esposa—the wife	el inglés—the Englishman
el día—the day	el hermano—the brother
el nombre—the name	los Estados Unidos—the United States
¿quién?—who?	rojo—red
recibir—to receive	para—for, in order to
¿cuál(es)?—which?	negro—black, Negro
sentado—seated	muy—very
americano—American	ahora—now
blanco—white	la fecha—the date
la hermana—the sister	la nacionalidad—the nationality

EXERCISE

1. Escriba Vd. la lección ahora. 2. El es mexicano pero está en los Estados Unidos. 3. El carro es para Vd. 4. (Yo) No estudio con él. 5. El alumno entra en el cuarto. 6. ¿Ha aprendido Vd. la lección? 7. ¿Quién es el hombre que está sentado allí? 8. Él tiene tres carros. 9. El río no es muy grande pero es muy largo. 10. Tengo un libro para mi papá. 11. ¿Cuál de los libros es para mí? 12. ¿Cuáles de las señoritas son las hermanas de Vd.? 13. Ella no va conmigo porque está enferma. 14. (Yo) Doy la pluma del niño a la muchacha. 15. ¿Quién va con nosotros? 16. La esposa de Carlos no está aquí.

EXERCISE

1. Write the exercise with pen and ink. 2. Which of the books on the table is for him? 3. Where do you live? 4. Do you study much? 5. The car is not here now. 6. The student receives many letters. 7. I study in order to learn. 8. I am well today, but John is sick. 9. The white hats are for us. 10. The man's wife is from Mexico. 11. What is your brother's occupation? 12. What is the nationality of the man with your brother? 13. Who is the man in the office? 14. Have you written to your mother? 15. The Englishman has received three letters from his wife.

POSSESSIVE ADJECTIVES (PRONOUNS)

Singular	Plural
mi—my	mis—my
tu—your[11]	tus—your[11]
su—his	sus—his
su—her	sus—her
su—your[11]	sus—your[11]
nuestro, a—our	nuestros, as—our
vuestro, a—your[11]	vuestros, as—your[11]
su—their	sus—their
su—their	sus—their
su—your[11]	sus—your[11]

In Spanish the possessive pronouns are considered by many grammarians as possessive adjectives and, like adjectives, they agree in gender and number with the thing possessed and not with the possessor.

Singular	Plural
mi sombrero—my hat	mis sombreros—my hats
mi pluma—my pen	mis plumas—my pens
nuestra casa—our house	nuestras casas—our houses
nuestro libro—our book	nuestros libros—our books
su primo—your cousin	sus primos—your cousins
su prima—your cousin	sus primas—your cousins

The possessive adjectives precede their noun and are repeated before each noun.

Carlos tiene mi libro y mis plumas.	Charles has my book and my pens.
Nuestra pluma y nuestro lápiz están en la mesa.	Our pen and our pencil are on the table.

Since "su" and "sus" can have so many meanings, in order to prevent ambiguity, it is often necessary to use the preposition "de" and the proper prepositional pronoun after the object possessed. When the prepositional pronoun is used for clearness, the definite article is generally substituted for the possessive adjective. Either form is correct, but the use of the definite article is preferable.

[11] The possessive adjectives corresponding to the English possessive pronoun "your" are expressed in four ways as listed above. "Tu" and "vuestro" are the familiar forms and "su" the polite form.

43

La casa de Vd.	Your house.
Su casa de Vd.	Your house.
Los libros de él.	His books.
Sus libros de él.	His books.
La tía de ellos.	Their aunt.
Su tía de ellos.	Their aunt.
Las tías de él.	His aunts.
Sus tías de él.	His aunts.

In the first two sentences below the possessor has already been given in the sentence and no ambiguity exists. In the third sentence "John" has the "book" of **"ella,"** another person; therefore, it is necessary to explain the sentence further with the prepositional phrase **"de ella."**

Juan tiene su libro.	John has his book.
Ella tiene su pluma.	She has her pen.
Juan tiene el libro de ella.	John has her book.

The masculine plural of nouns and of adjectives used as nouns may include both male and female beings when they denote rank or relation: **"Los niños,"** the children, the boy and the girl, the boys and the girls, or the boys. Should there be any ambiguity in meaning the noun may be repeated: **"El niño y la niña."**

los abuelos—the grandparents	los niños—the children
los alumnos—the students	los padres—the parents
los hermanos—the brothers and sisters	los tíos—the uncle and aunt
los jóvenes—the young (people)	los ricos—the rich (people)
los viejos—the old (people)	los pobres—the poor (people)
	los ancianos—the old (people)

VOCABULARY

hermosa—beautiful	pagar—to pay
el oficial—the officer, the official	amarillo—yellow
¿cuánto?—how much?	abrir—to open
el tío—the uncle	la ventana—the window
la tía—the aunt	si—if
cada—each, every	el primo—the cousin
varios—various, several	la prima—the cousin
varias—various, several	verde—green
el abuelo—the grandfather	azul—blue
la abuela—the grandmother	el hermano—the brother
Eduardo—Edward	la hermana—the sister

EXERCISE

1. Mi esposa no vive en México. 2. ¿Cuántos niños tiene Vd.? 3. ¿Viven los tíos de Vd. en El Paso? 4. Él estudia su lección cada día. 5. ¿Desea Vd. comprar el carro de Eduardo? 6. Nosotros bebemos (tomamos)

agua. 7. Nuestra casa es blanca y está en la calle Elm. 8. ¿Ha recibido Vd. una carta de su primo? 9. Sí, señor, he recibido cinco cartas de mi primo. 10. Juan tiene un sombrero nuevo. 11. La casa de Juan no es muy hermosa. 12. ¿Qué desea Vd.? 13. Yo no he comido. 14. ¿En dónde están los jóvenes hoy? 15. ¿Qué ha comprado Juan?

EXERCISE

1. Where is your husband? 2. My uncle and aunt live in the United States. 3. How much do you study every day? 4. The young lady is very beautiful. 5. His children are young. 6. Open the door. 7. The lady's hat is not new. 8. His family does not live in Mexico. 9. Their children are in California. 10. Do you drink much water? 11. Why don't you study your lessons every night? 12. The children do not study very much. 13. How many letters have you received from your grandmother? 14. How many windows are there in the room? 15. In what city does your brother live?

THE POSSESSIVE PRONOUNS

Sing.	Plural	Sing.	Plural	English
el mío	los míos	la mía	las mías	mine
el tuyo	los tuyos	la tuya	las tuyas	yours
el suyo	los suyos	la suya	las suyas	his
el suyo	los suyos	la suya	las suyas	hers
el suyo	los suyos	la suya	las suyas	yours
el nuestro	los nuestros	la nuestra	las nuestras	ours
el vuestro	los vuestros	la vuestra	las vuestras	yours
el suyo	los suyos	la suya	las suyas	theirs
el suyo	los suyos	la suya	las suyas	theirs
el suyo	los suyos	la suya	las suyas	yours

A possessive pronoun agrees with the noun for which it stands in gender and number.

In the following sentences the word **"libro"** has been replaced by the possessive pronoun. **"Libro"** is masculine singular; therefore, the masculine singular possessive pronoun has replaced it.

¿Dónde está su libro?	Where is your book?
El mío está aquí.	Mine is here.
El suyo es verde.	His is green.
El nuestro es grande.	Ours is large.

In the following sentences the word **"pluma"** is feminine singular and is replaced by the feminine singular possessive pronoun.

Esta pluma es verde.	This pen is green.
La mía no es blanca.	Mine is not white.
La suya es negra.	Hers is black.
La nuestra es grande.	Ours is large.

In the following sentences the word **"libros"** is masculine plural and is replaced by the masculine plural possessive pronoun.

¿En dónde están sus libros?	Where are your books?
Los míos están aquí.	Mine are here.
Los suyos son rojos.	His are red.
Los nuestros son rojos.	Ours are red.

In the following sentences the word **"plumas"** is feminine plural, and, therefore, is replaced by the feminine plural possessive pronoun.

Estas plumas son verdes.	These pens are green.
Las mías son blancas.	Mine are white.
Las suyas son negras.	Hers are black.
Las nuestras son grandes.	Ours are large.

In order to prevent ambiguity, instead of **"el suyo"** use **"el de él,"** **"el de ella,"** **"el de Vd.,"** etc. Instead of **"la suya"** use **"la de él,"** **"la de ella,"** **"la de Vd.,"** etc. Instead of **"los suyos"** use **"los de él,"** **"los de ella,"** **"los de Vd.,"** etc. Instead of **"las suyas"** use **"las de él,"** **"las de ella,"** **"las de Vd.,"** etc.

Tengo el suyo =

Tengo el de él.	I have his.
Tengo el de ella.	I have hers.
Tengo el de Vd.	I have yours.
Tengo el de ellos.	I have theirs.
Tengo el de ellas.	I have theirs.
Tengo el de Vds.	I have yours.

In order to prevent the repetition of the noun, the following construction may be used:

Mi pluma y la pluma de Juan.	My pen and John's pen.
Mi pluma y la de Juan.	My pen and John's.
Su lápiz y el lápiz de María.	Your pencil and Mary's pencil.
Su lápiz y el de María.	Your pencil and Mary's.

Immediately following the verb **"ser"** the definite article may be omitted. However, it may be used for emphasis.

Este libro es el suyo.	This book is yours. (emphasis)
Este libro es suyo.	This book is yours.
Esta pluma es la suya.	This pen is his. (emphasis)
Esta pluma es suya.	This pen is his.
La pluma es la de él.	The pen is his. (emphasis)
La pluma es de él.	The pen is his.
La pluma es la de Juan.	The pen is John's. (emphasis)
La pluma es de Juan.	The pen is John's.

The possessive pronoun is sometimes used after a noun and is usually translated "of mine," "of his," etc., or "my" if used in an exclamation.

Un amigo mío me lo dió.	A friend of mine gave it to me.
¡Hijo mío! ¡Qué alto es Vd.!	My son! How tall you are!
Un hermano suyo murió.	A brother of his died.
Or: Su hermano murió.	His brother died.

VOCABULARY

el vino—the wine	el café—the coffee
la leche—the milk	la cerveza—the beer

en casa—at home (location)
a casa—(to) home (motion)
corto—short
alto—tall, high

otro—other, another
manejar—to drive
guiar—to guide, drive
cruzar—to cross

IRREGULAR PAST PARTICIPLES

Infinitive	Past Participle
escribir—to write	escrito—written
abrir—to open	abierto—open(ed)
hacer—to make, do	hecho—made, done
decir—to say, tell	dicho—said, told
volver—to return	vuelto—returned
ver—to see	vista—seen
poner—to place, put	puesto—placed, put
romper—to tear	roto—torn
morir—to die	muerto—dead
cubrir—to cover	cubierto—covered

No attempt has been made to list all verbs with irregular past participles; however, those most commonly encountered are listed.

EXERCISE

1. Mis libros están en la mesa; los suyos no están aquí. 2. Esta pluma es roja; la de Juan es blanca. 3. Yo he vendido la casa de María; no he vendido la de Vd. 4. Las casas de Vd. son verdes; las mías son blancas. 5. Tengo el lápiz de Juan; no tengo el de María. 6. Un amigo mío ha comprado una pluma roja. 7. Vd. no ha aprendido su lección. 8. ¿Quién es el hombre? 9. Juan tiene el libro de ella; no tiene el mío. 10. ¿Ha escrito él una carta a su madre? 11. Sí, pero él no ha recibido las cartas de la madre de ella. 12. El pasaporte de ella está aquí. 13. ¿Dónde está el mío? Está en la mesa. 14. Este sombrero es mío; el otro es de Juan. 15. Hay muchos libros en la mano de él.

EXERCISE

1. He doesn't drink much water. 2. Where are your children now? 3. This passport is not mine; it is my son's. 4. The pen is hers and the pencil is his. 5. Her son is young, but he is very large. 6. Who is this boy? 7. He is my uncle's son. 8. What are you studying? 9. I am writing a letter to his sister. 10. John's pen and mine are here. 11. Are his children here? 12. His are here, but hers are not. 13. Write a letter to Mary's father. 14. Where is my aunt? 15. Your aunt is from Mexico, but she is here now.

LESSON X

DEMONSTRATIVE ADJECTIVES AND PRONOUNS

	Singular				Plural		
Masc.	Eng.	Fem.		Masc.	Eng.	Fem.
este	this	esta	near speaker	estos	these	estas
ese	that	esa	near spoken to	esos	those	esas
aquel	that	aquella	at a distance	aquellos	those	aquellas

The demonstrative adjective precedes the noun that it modifies and agrees with it in number and gender.

esta pluma	this pen	estas plumas	these pens
este libro	this book	estos libros	these books
esa carta	that letter	esas cartas	those letters
ese libro	that book	esos libros	those books
aquella pluma	that pen	aquellas plumas	those pens
aquel libro	that book	aquellos libros	those books

When the demonstratives stand alone, they take the place of the object pointed out and bear the written accent mark over the vowel of the proper syllable. When they stand alone they are demonstrative pronouns. The pronouns agree in number and gender with the nouns whose place they take.

Éste es mi libro.	This is my book.
Ése es (el) mío.	That is mine.
Éstas son de mi padre.	These are my father's.
¿De quién es éste?	Whose is this?

The neuter pronouns "esto," "eso," and "aquello" have no written accent mark and are used when the thing for which they stand is a statement, idea, or something indefinite or unknown.

¿Qué es esto?	What is this?
Eso no es verdad.	That is not true.
¡Eso es!	That's it!
No quiero pensar en aquello.	I don't want to think of that.

THE PRESENT INDICATIVE TENSE OF "HACER," "DECIR," AND "VENIR"

Hacer (to do, make)		Decir (to say, tell)		Venir (to come)	
hago	hacemos	digo	decimos	vengo	venimos
haces	hacéis	dices	decís	vienes	venís
hace	hacen	dice	dicen	viene	vienen

49

ADJECTIVES OF NATIONALITY

Adjectives of nationality form the feminine by changing "o" to "a" or if they end in a consonant by adding "a" to the masculine singular form. They are also used as nouns.

un hombre español	a Spanish man
una mujer española	a Spanish woman
un hombre mexicano	a Mexican man
una mujer mexicana	a Mexican woman
el español	the Spaniard
la española	the Spanish woman
el inglés	the Englishman
la inglesa	the Engishwoman

"ACÁ," "AQUÍ," "AHÍ," "ALLÁ," AND "ALLÍ"

"Acá" is generally used instead of "aquí" meaning "here" with verbs of motion. "Ahí" means "there" near the person spoken to; "allí" means "there" in a definite place remote from both speaker and person spoken to; "allá" is used meaning "there" after verbs of motion and also means "there" or "yonder" in an indefinite place.

este hombre aquí	this man here (near speaker)
venga Vd. acá	come here (motion)
ese hombre ahí	that man there (near you)
aquel hombre allí	that man there (definite place)
ellos fueron allá	they went there (over yonder)

USE OF DEFINITE ARTICLE BEFORE THE NAME OF A LANGUAGE

In Spanish the definite article is used before the name of a language except immediately after the verb "hablar" or the preposition "en."

Yo estudio el español.	I study Spanish.
Yo hablo español.	I speak Spanish.
Yo hablo bien el inglés.	I speak English well.
Está escrito en inglés.	It[12] is written in English.

VOCABULARY

el inglés—English	el permiso—the permit
el español—Spanish	el patrón—the boss
inglés (adj.)—English	el caballo—the horse
español (adj.)—Spanish	la semana—the week
la vaca—the cow	el trabajo—the work

[12] "It" as a subject pronoun is not generally written or said, but is understood.

la tarjeta—the card	**gastar**—to spend
local—local	**ganar**—to earn, win
firmar—to sign	**desear**—to desire
derecho—right	**aquí**—here
izquierdo—left	**acá**—here
la ciudad—the city	**allí**—there
todo (adj.)—all	**ahí**—there
trabajar—to work	**allá**—there

EXERCISE

1. ¿Dónde está el permiso de Vd.? 2. (Yo) He gastado todo el dinero. 3. No hay mucho trabajo en México. 4. Mi pasaporte está allí en la mesa. 5. ¿Qué hace Vd.? 6. El caballo es de mi padre. 7. ¿Habla Vd. español? 8. Una semana tiene siete días. 9. (Yo) No gano mucho dinero. 10. Su padre trabaja en El Paso, pero el mío no trabaja allí. 11. ¿Está Vd. cansado? 12. (Yo) No estoy cansado pero estoy malo. 13. (Yo) No he vendido las plumas de él. 14. Él no habla inglés; es de México.

EXERCISE

1. That man works here. 2. They work a great deal. 3. Those women are his aunts. 4. These passports are new. 5. They don't buy many things. 6. There are many children on the street. 7. No, she doesn't have (any) work now. 8. This man is her uncle. 9. Is this woman your aunt? 10. All the pens are mine. 11. There is a mole on his right hand. 12. Do you earn much money now? 13. Those white pencils are yours. 14. Is this book yours?

THE PAST INDICATIVE TENSES

In Spanish there are two past indicative tenses: the *preterite indicative*, and the *imperfect indicative*. They are not used interchangeably.

THE PRETERITE INDICATIVE TENSE – past

To conjugate verbs in the preterite indicative, attach the following endings to the stem of the verb:

"AR" verbs: é, aste, ó, amos, asteis, aron
"ER" verbs: í, iste, ió, imos, isteis, ieron
"IR" verbs: í, iste, ió, imos, isteis, ieron,

Hablar	Comer	Recibir
habl-é	com-í	recib-í
habl-aste	com-iste	recib-iste
habl-ó	com-ió	recib-ió
habl-amos	com-imos	recib-imos
habl-asteis	com-isteis	recib-isteis
habl-aron	com-ieron	recib-ieron

The preterite indicative tense is used to express definitely completed past action. It is called by some grammarians the past absolute, past definite, or historical past. The preterite simply calls attention to completed action in past time.

Juan comió aquí ayer.	John ate here yesterday.
María compró un carro el mes pasado.	Mary bought a car last month.
¿Cuándo entró Vd. en México?	When did you enter Mexico?
¿En dónde compró Vd. este libro?	Where did you buy this book?
¿Vendió él su pluma?	Did he sell his pen?

THE IMPERFECT INDICATIVE TENSE – NOT AT AN EXACT TIME

To conjugate verbs in the imperfect indicative, attach the following endings to the stem of the verb:

"AR" verbs: aba, abas, aba, ábamos, abais, aban
"ER" verbs: ía, ías, ía, íamos, íais, ían
"IR" verbs: ía, ías, ía, íamos, íais, ían

Hablar	Comer	Recibir
habl-aba	com-ía	recib-ía
habl-abas	com-ías	recib-ías
habl-aba	com-ía	recib-ía
habl-ábamos	com-íamos	recib-íamos
habl-abais	com-íais	recib-íais
habl-aban	com-ían	recib-ían

There are only three verbs that are irregular in the imperfect indicative tense.

Ser: era, eras, era, éramos, erais, eran ~~perm.~~ | ~~Estar not perm.~~
Ir: iba, ibas, iba, íbamos, ibais, iban
Ver: veía, veías, veía, veíamos, veíais, veían

The imperfect indicative tense is used:

(1) To express customary or habitual past action. This corresponds to the English "used" followed by an infinitive (used to eat).

Yo comía allí cada día.
I used to eat there every day.

Él ganaba mucho dinero en México.
He used to earn much money in Mexico.

María escribía muchas cartas a su madre.
Mary used to write many letters to her mother.

Yo estudiaba cada día cuando vivía en El Paso.
I studied every day when I lived in El Paso.

(2) To express interrupted past action. In this case the interrupted action—that which was going on—is placed in the imperfect indicative, and the interrupting action—that which did the interrupting—is put in the preterite indicative. The imperfect action is generally expressed by the progressive imperfect (imperfect of **"estar"** plus the present participle of the main verb). *See* page 64, Progressive Action.

Anoche (yo) estaba estudiando (estudiaba) cuando Carlos entró.
Last night I was studying when Charles entered.

Pablo estaba hablando (hablaba) a María cuando entré en el cuarto.
Paul was talking to Mary when I entered the room.

(3) To express two or more actions going along together. All of these actions will be put in the imperfect and either the simple imperfect or the progressive imperfect (most general) may be used. (Notice that the translation in these cases is "was" or "were" plus the present participle in English.)

Yo estaba trabajando (trabajaba), y ella estaba leyendo (leía) el periódico.
I was working, and she was reading the newspaper.

Enrique estaba escribiendo (escribía) una carta, y su esposa estaba preparando (preparaba) la comida.
Henry was writing a letter, and his wife was preparing dinner.

José estaba hablando (hablaba), pero Juan no estaba escuchando (escuchaba).
Joseph was talking, but John was not listening.

VERBS IRREGULAR IN THE PRETERITE INDICATIVE

There are 17 verbs that are irregular in the preterite indicative tense, and at first glance this may seem to be a very difficult tense due to the irregularities. However, 14 of these verbs, although possessing irregular stems, take the same irregular preterite endings as follow: e, iste, o, imos, isteis, ieron.

In these 14 verbs those ending in "j" drop the "i" of the "ieron" ending: **condujeron, dijeron, trajeron.** In the third person singular **"hacer"** changes the "c" to "z" before "o" to retain the original soft "c" sound.

Infinitive	**Irregular stem**	Meaning
andar	anduv	to walk
estar	estuv	to be
haber	hub	to have (aux.)
hacer	hic	to do, make
poder	pud	to be able
poner	pus	to put, place
tener	tuv	to have
venir	vin	to come
querer	quis	to wish, want
saber	sup	to know (how)
traer	traj	to bring
decir	dij	to say, tell
caber	cup	to fit into
conducir	conduj	to conduct, lead

"Ser" (to be) and **"ir"** (to go) are conjugated alike in the preterite; **fuí, fuiste, fué, fuimos, fuisteis, fueron.**

"Dar" (to give) is conjugated like a regular "er" verb in the preterite: **dí, diste, dió, dimos, disteis, dieron.**

Any verb of the second and third conjugation whose stem ends in a vowel changes the unaccented "i" between vowels to "y," as an unaccented "i" may not appear between vowels in Spanish:

Le-er: le-í, le-íste, le-yó, le-ímos, le-ísteis, le-yeron
Ca-er: ca-í, ca-íste, ca-yó, ca-ímos, ca-ísteis, ca-yeron

The "i" of the second person singular and of the first and second persons plural is accented in order to break what would otherwise be a diphthong.

54

Many verbs appear to be irregular in the preterite, but are only ortho-graphically (spelling) so. The change in spelling is made in order to retain the sound of the final consonant of the stem of the verb. Verbs ending in "car" change the "c" to "qu" before "e" in order to retain the "k" sound. Verbs ending in "gar" change "g" to "gu." (*See* pages 136 to 138.)

Buscar: **busqué, buscaste, buscó,** etc.
Pagar: **pagué, pagaste, pagó,** etc.

Radical changing verbs (*see* page 100) of the second and third classi-fications make certain changes in the stem of the verb.

VOCABULARY

ayer—yesterday
anoche—last night
mañana—morning, tomorrow
esta mañana—this morning
legal—legal, lawful
hace—it makes (ago)
salir—to leave
regresar—to return
la verdad—the truth
brincar—to jump
la tienda—the store
la milla—the mile
la línea—the line
el pueblo—the town
la garita—the entrance gate
el inspector—the inspector
ver—to see
escuchar—to listen
poner—to put
el desierto—the desert
el tiempo—the time

cruzar—to cross
la semana pasada—last week
el año—the year
el año pasado—last year
el mes—the month
perder—to lose
el abuelo—the grandfather
la abuela—the grandmother
buscar—to look for, seek
el dólar—the dollar (Amer.)
el peso—the dollar (Mex.)
el teléfono—the telephone
el comerciante—the merchant
el periódico—the newspaper
preparar—to prepare
la oficina—the office
la botella—the bottle
cerca de—near
por—by, through, for
ilegal—illegal, unlawful
local—local

EXERCISE

1. Ayer él anduvo a pie al pueblo conmigo. 2. Anita no vino de México con su madre porque estaba mala cuando salió su madre. 3. ¿En dónde puso Vd. su sombrero cuando regresó a casa anoche? 4. ¿Cuando vini-eron sus abuelos de Hermosillo? 5. No pude hacer el trabajo ayer por la mañana. 6. Cuando (yo) vivía en El Centro, veía a mis padres cada semana. 7. ¿Qué estaba haciendo (hacía) José ayer cuando Vd. pasó por su casa (de él)? 8. ¿Qué estaba haciendo (hacía) Vd. ayer cuando mi primo fué a su casa? 9. Yo estaba escribiendo una carta y él estaba leyendo el periódico. 10. Cuántas millas anduvo (viajó) Vd. por el de-

sierto? 11. Él no llegó a tiempo anoche. 12. Carlota escribió una carta a su padre ayer. 13. El comerciante no vendió mucho el año pasado. 14. La mujer mandó cinco dólares a su hija. 15. ¿Qué estaba haciendo (hacía) Vd. ayer en la oficina cuando entré? 16. Yo estaba buscando (buscaba) mi pasaporte que perdí ayer por la mañana. (yesterday morning.) 17. El carro no costó mucho dinero. 18. No he vendido muchos periódicos este año. 19. Él veía a mi hijo cada día cuando vivía cerca de mí en Nogales. 20. ¿Cuántos años vivieron sus padres en Sonora, México?

EXERCISE

1. How many miles did you walk? 2. I sold many newspapers yesterday. 3. Why didn't you go to the office this morning? 4. What were you buying in the store when I passed? 5. I was buying a hat from[14] the merchant. 6. She was talking, but the boy was not listening. 7. When I lived in Los Angeles, I worked all the time. 8. I used to live in Mexico, but I have been living in Texas for ten years. 9. There is no telephone at my home. 10. Do you live near this man? 11. Where were you going when you saw our car? 12. I was going to visit my son.

N.B. When the direct object noun is a definitely known person or an intelligent animal, it is generally preceded by the preposition "a."

Visité a mis amigos.	I visited my friends.
No he visto a María.	I have not seen Mary.
Vendí a Whirlaway.	I sold Whirlaway.
But: **Busco un caballo.**	I am looking for a horse.

"**Tener**" does not take "a" before its object:

Tengo dos hermanos.	I have two brothers.

[14] "Comprar" and "pedir" require "a" instead of "de" before their objects.

Compré el libro al comericante.	I bought the book from the merchant.
Pedí dinero a mi padre.	I asked my father for money.

TIME EXPRESSIONS

The verb **"ser"** is always used in telling time. The words **"hora"** (o'clock) and **"minutos"** (minutes) are understood. The verb agrees with the hour in number and person. The number expressing the hour is preceded by the definite article, which agrees with the word **"hora"** in number and gender. **"Media"** (half) is an adjective and **"cuarto"** (quarter) is a noun.

To express fractional time, the hour and the number of minutes past the hour are joined by the conjunction **"y"**. In the spoken language, minutes beyond the half hour are often expressed by subtracting them from the following hour by use of the word **"menos."** To express "a.m." add **"de la mañana"** to the time expression. To express "P.M." add **de la tarde"** or **"de la noche,"** as appropriate, to the time expression.

There are several ways of telling time. The beginner will do well to use one until completely familiar with it before attempting others.

What time is?	**¿Qué hora es?**
It is 1:00 o'clock.	**Es la una.**
It is 2:00 o'clock.	**Son las dos.**
It is 5:30 o'clock.	**Son las cinco y media.**
It is 7:15 o'clock.	**Son las siete y quince.**
It is 7:15 o'clock.	**Son las siete y cuarto.**
It is 8:50 o'clock.	**Son las nueve menos diez.**
It is 9:55 o'clock.	**Son las diez menos cinco.**
It is noon.	**Es mediodía.**
It is noon.	**Son las doce del día.**
It is midnight.	**Son las doce de la noche.**
It is midnight.	**Es medianoche.**
It is 6:00 o'clock sharp.	**Son las seis en punto.**
It is 8:00 A.M.	**Son las ocho de la mañana.**
It is 3:00 P.M.	**Son las tres de la tarde.**
It is 11:00 P.M.	**Son las once de la noche.**
At what time?	**¿A qué hora?**
At 10:00 P.M.	**A las diez de la noche.**
In the morning.	**Por la mañana.**
In the afternoon.	**Por la tarde.**

"HACER" IN TIME EXPRESSIONS

"**Hacer**" is used in time expressions to show an elapse of time between two events or periods of time.

Hace diez años que vivo aquí.	I have lived here for ten years. (It makes ten years that I live here.)
Hace cinco días que yo le ví a él. **Yo le ví hace cinco días.**	I saw him five days ago. (It makes five days since I saw him.)
Mañana hará tres semanas que he estado en El Paso.	Tomorrow I shall have been in El Paso three weeks. (Tomorrow will make three weeks that I have been in El Paso.)
Él llegó ayer; hacía diez años que no le habíamos visto.	He arrived yesterday; we had not seen him for ten years.

CALENDAR DIVISIONS

Months of the year		*Days of the week*	
enero	January	**el domingo**	Sunday
febrero	February	**el lunes**	Monday
marzo	March	**el martes**	Tuesday
abril	April	**el miércoles**	Wednesday
mayo	May	**el jueves**	Thursday
junio	June	**el viernes**	Friday
julio	July	**el sábado**	Saturday
agosto	August	*Seasons of the year*	
septiembre	September	**la primavera**	spring
octubre	October	**el verano**	summer
noviembre	November	**el otoño**	autumn
diciembre	December	**el invierno**	winter

There are several ways of asking the date, month, or day of the month:

¿Qué día del mes es hoy? **¿Qué día del mes tenemos?** **¿A cuántos estamos?** **¿A cómo estamos?**	What day of the month is it?
¿Cuál es la fecha (de hoy)? **¿Qué fecha tenemos?**	What is the date?
¿En qué mes estamos? **¿Qué mes es éste?**	What month is this?

VOCABULARY

el café—café, coffee
la iglesia—the church
la noche—the night

la tarde—the afternoon
tarde—late
Es tarde.—It is late.

temprano—early	**El año nuevo**—New Year's Day
Es temprano.—It is early.	**la nochebuena**—Christmas Eve
el año—the year	**la madrugada**—early morning
el año pasado—last year	**la madrugada**—the dawn
el mes—the month	**anteanoche**—night before last
la hora—the hour	**hace**—it makes (ago)
Jorge—George	**¿cuándo?**—when?
último—last	**a la madrugada**—at dawn, at an early hour
el periódico—the newspaper	**a la caída de la tarde**—at nightfall
día festivo—holiday	**mañana por la tarde**—tomorrow afternoon
día de fiesta—holiday	**mañana por la mañana**—tomorrow morning
día de descanso—rest day	**pasado mañana**—day after tomorrow
día de trabajo—work day	**pasado mañana**—(lit.) the day past to-
día de Navidad—Christmas	morrow
mañana por la noche—tomorrow	**ayer por la tarde**—yesterday afternoon
night	**ayer por la mañana**—yesterday morning
esta noche—tonight	**ahora**—now
ayer—yesterday	**el diario**—the newspaper
anteayer—day before yesterday	**ahorita**—right now
la semana entrante—next week	**ahora mismo**—right now
ocho días—eight days (week)	**rato**—short while (time)
quincena—fortnight	**el minuto**—the minute
la semana próxima—next week	**ratito**—short while (time)
próxima—next	**medio**—half
la semana que viene—next week	**cuarto**—fourth, quarter
de noche—by night	**media hora**—half hour
de día—by day	**en punto**—sharp (on the dot)
el anochecer—dusk	**siglo**—century
el amanecer—dawn, daybreak	**tener que** + infinitive—to have to
como—like, as	**cuando**—when
día de año nuevo—New Year's Day	**quince días**—two weeks

EXERCISE

1. ¿A qué hora entró Vd. anoche? 2. (Yo) Entré a las seis de la tarde. 3. (Yo) Compré el periódico ayer por la tarde. 4. Voy a El Paso mañana por la mañana. 5. ¿Cuándo estudian Vds.? 6. ¿Sabe Vd. a qué hora salió su primo anoche? 7. Por qué iba Vd. a Nogales? 8. Son las siete y media de la noche. 9. Es tarde, ¿(en) dónde ha estado Vd.? 10. Él llegó a las nueve en punto. 11. Son las cuatro y media y mi hija no ha vuelto del hotel.

EXERCISE

1. What did you do last night? 2. Day before yesterday we went to church with our cousin George. 3. He arrived at midnight. 4. Night before last I saw Mary with her friend. 5. Was it early or late when you came in last night? 6. What time was it this morning when I talked to you

on the phone **(por teléfono)**? 7. We left the town at nightfall. 8. What are you going to do on New Year's Day? 9. I do not work in the afternoon. 10. Tomorrow morning my uncle and I are going to Las Cruces. 11. Our parents are not ill now. 12. My brother and his wife went to Acapulco last week.

COMPARISON OF THE PRESENT PERFECT
AND THE PRETERITE TENSES

Present perfect indicative		*Preterite indicative*	
Yo he comido.	I have eaten.	Yo comí.	I ate.
Él ha salido.	He has gone.	Él salió.	He left.
Hemos hablado.	We have spoken.	Hablamos.	We spoke.
Ellos han comido.	They have eaten.	Ellos comieron.	They ate.

As can be seen in the examples above (the present perfect and the preterite), the actions expressed are already terminated. In the present perfect the action is completed, but the time expressed is present. In the preterite, the action and the time are both past. The present perfect is used if the action in question takes place within a space of time not yet expired, such as this day, this week, this month, this year, etc., or at an indefinite time in any way connected with the present. However, if the time of day (hour) at which the action took place is stated with the word "today" and is past, then the preterite and not the present perfect is used. Study the following examples very closely.

¿Ha visto Vd. a Juan hoy?	Have you seen John today?
¿Cuántas cartas ha recibido su mamá esta semana?	How many letters has your mother received this week?
He estudiado mucho este año.	I have studied very much this year.
¿Ha viajado Vd. mucho por México?	Have you traveled much in Mexico?
Los ingleses han construido muchos vapores.	The English have constructed many ships.
María ha leído muchos libros.	Mary has read many books.
Hoy yo comí a las cuatro de la tarde.	Today I ate dinner (dined) at 4:00 P.M.
Él me vió esta mañana a las diez.	He saw me this morning at ten o'clock.
Carlos llegó esta tarde a las dos.	Charles arrived this afternoon at two o'clock.
Edison hizo muchas invenciones.	Edison made many inventions.
El Presidente Wilson escribió muchos libros.	President Wilson wrote many books.
El Presidente Lincoln viajó mucho.	President Lincoln traveled a great deal.
María escribió tres cartas ayer.	Mary wrote three letters yesterday.
Juan ganó mucho dinero el año pasado.	John earned much money last year.
Estudié tres horas anoche.	I studied three hours last night.

61

In the above examples, in the first group the time is present and the action completed within that period of time. In the second group, although the time is not definitely expressed, the action is definitely connected with the present in that these actions could continue to happen; the person still exists and may do these actions in the future. In the third group, although the time is expressed as the present period, a specific past hour is expressed during the present time, thereby making the sentence definitely past, and the preterite tense is used. In the fourth group, although the time is not expressed, the actions are definitely past, because the doers of these actions are dead, thereby cutting off any possibility of their doing the actions again. In the last group the time expressed is definitely past and so are the actions.

THE POLITE REQUEST AND "THANK YOU"

There are several ways of expressing "please" in Spanish. Study the examples and their translations given below:

Tenga Vd. la bondad de dármelo.	Have the goodness to give it to me.
Hágame Vd. el favor de dármelo.	Do me the favor to give (of giving) it to me.
Sírvase Vd. dármelo.	Please give it to me.
Démelo Vd. por favor.	Give it to me, please.

All of the above translate: "Please give it to me."
There are several ways of expressing "thank you" in Spanish:

Muchas gracias.	Many thanks.
Muchísimas gracias.	Many, many thanks.
Mil gracias or	A thousand thanks.
Un millón de gracias.	A thousand thanks.
No hay de qué. (Lit.: There is no cause why.)	You are welcome. (Don't mention it.)
De nada or por nada or no es nada.	It is nothing. You are welcome.

VOCABULARY

ya—already	la llegada—the arrival
el traje—the suit	solicitar—to solicit, ask for
el vestido—the dress	pedir—to ask for
la ropa—the clothes	la inmigración—the immigration
el vapor—the ship	la vez—time (counting)
el buque—the boat	viajar—to travel
el lugar—the place	bajar (de)—to lower, get out of
el sitio—the site	subir (a)—to climb, get into
todavía—yet	todavía no—not yet
al otro lado—on the other side	el recibo—the receipt
llegar—to arrive	la visa—the visa
acabar—to finish, end	el lado—the side
el teatro—the theater	siempre—always

1. ¿Cuánto tiempo ha estado Vd. en México? 2. ¿Cuántas cartas ha recibido Vd. de su mamá esta semana? 3. Recibí dos cartas la semana pasada y he recibido tres esta semana. 4. ¿En dónde compró Vd. ese sombrero? 5. Compré este sombrero en la tienda de Smith. 6. Ví a María esta mañana a las ocho pero no he visto a Juan todavía. 7. ¿Ha solicitado (pedido) Vd. una visa de inmigración? 8. Pedí (solicité) una visa de inmigración el mes pasado. 9. Nunca he estado en los Estados Unidos antes. 10. Siempre he vivido al otro lado. 11. Fuí a visitar a mi abuela pero ella no estaba en casa. 12. ¿Ha estado Vd. alguna vez en el Estado de Colorado? 13. ¿Adónde fué Vd. anoche?

1. Have you written (to) your friend this week? 2. I wrote three letters to John last month. 3. Have you finished the work on that ranch? 4. I have already worked there for two months, and my brother is working there now. 5. I bought this hat from a boy in Juarez for (por) ten pesos. 6. He told me that it was his. 7. When did your grandfather arrive in Juarez? 8. He has not arrived yet; he is still in Chihuahua City.

PROGRESSIVE ACTION

The present participle of a verb is formed by adding "ando" to the stem of "AR" verbs and "iendo" to the stem of "ER" and "IR" verbs:

> **hablar—hablando** (speaking)
> **comer—comiendo** (eating)
> **vivir—viviendo** (living)

The present tense of the verb **"estar"** is used before the present participle of a verb to express progressive action in the present time.

> **Él está hablando.**   He is speaking.
> **(Yo) Estoy comiendo.**   I am eating.

The present indicative tense may be used instead of the present progressive, but it is not as forceful, nor is it commonly used to express a progressive action.

The imperfect tense of the verb **"estar"** is used before the present participle of a verb to show progressive action in past time. This action may also be expressed by the imperfect tense of the main verb.

> **Ella estaba trabajando.**   She was working.
> **Vds. estaban estudiando.**   You were studying.

PRESENT INDICATIVE TENSE OF "SALIR" AND "PONER"

Salir (to leave)		Poner (to put, place)	
salgo	salimos	pongo	ponemos
sales	salís	pones	ponéis
sale	salen	pone	ponen

"PARA" AND "POR"

Para is used:

1. To show destination, purpose, or use.

Él sale para Nuevo York.   He is leaving for New York.
¿Para dónde va Vd.?   (For) Where are you going?
El libro es para Vd.   The book is for you.

Estudio para aprender.	I study in order to learn.
Él estudia para médico.	He is studying to be a doctor.
Ella tiene un vaso para vino.	She has a wine glass.
Tengo veinte dólares para ropa.	I have twenty dollars for clothes.

2. To express a point in future time.

La lección para mañana es fácil.	The lesson for tomorrow is easy.
Él tiene una cita para el lunes.	He has an appointment (date) for Monday.

Por is used:

1. To denote an agent (*see* passive voice, page 96).

El libro fué escrito por este hombre.	The book was written by this man.

2. To express source (by, through, for, or along).

Él entró por la puerta.	He entered through the door.
¿Por dónde pasó Vd.?	Where did you enter (pass)?
Trabajo por (con) el señor Blanco.	I work for Mr. White.
Él va por el médico.	He is going for the doctor.
Lo hice por Vd.	I did it for you (for your sake).
Viajamos por México.	We traveled through Mexico.

3. To express exchange:

Él pagó cinco pesos por el sombrero.	He paid five pesos for the hat.
(Yo) He dado mi sombrero por el libro.	I have given my hat for the book.

4. To express a unit of measure or number:

Gano dos pesos por día (al día).	I earn two pesos a day (per day).
Se venden por docena.	They are sold by the dozen.
Diez por ciento de los hombres fueron allá.	Ten percent of the men went there.

5. To express a period of time:

He trabajado aquí por dos meses.	I have worked here for two months.
Él ha vivido aquí por mucho tiempo.	He has lived here for a long time.

VOCABULARY

el norte—the north	**a la izquierda**—to the left
el sur—the south	**la cita**—the date, appointment
el este—the east	**conseguir**—to obtain, get
el oeste—the west	**delante (de)**—before, in front of
el vaso—the glass	**adelante**—ahead, forward
a pie—on foot	**adelante de**—ahead of
el médico—the doctor	**después**—after, next, later
el doctor—the doctor	**entre**—between, among
al derecho—straight ahead	**después (de) que**—after
a la derecha—to the right	**bajo** (adj.)—low, short

bajo (adv.)—under, below
abajo (adv.)—under, below, down
debajo de—under, beneath
cerca (de)—near
lejos (de)—far
dentro (de)—inside, within
fuera (de)—out, outside
de fuera—from the outside
por fuera—on the outside

detrás (de)—behind, after
atrás—behind, backward, back
atrás de—behind, back of
antes de—before
antes—before, formerly
antes (de) que—before
después de—after
entregar—to hand, deliver

EXERCISE

1. Juan está estudiando para médico. 2. María pagó cinco dólares por su sombrero. 3. El hombre salió para Cuba. 4. El muchacho y su primo están estudiando la lección para mañana. 5. (Yo) Deseo trabajar para ganar más dinero. 6. Mi hermano no ha vivido en México antes. 7. Él estaba trabajando por mi madre cuando recibió la carta. 8. Él está detrás de la mesa. 9. ¿Cuánto tiempo ha vivido Vd. aquí? 10. ¿Vive Vd. cerca de este hombre? No, señor, vivo lejos de él. 11. Después que vino él, salimos para Cuba. 12. El hombre está dentro de la casa. 13. Vivo a la derecha de aquella casa. 14. Antes de[15] entrar conseguí un pasaporte.

EXERCISE

1. He has not lived here before. 2. What did the inspector say yesterday? 3. After[15] entering the United States, I left for Colorado. 4. This letter is for you. 5. Do you live near your uncle? 6. What did you do next? 7. I visited my uncle who lives near there. 8. Her father says that John is rich. 9. When did you receive this letter? 10. I received the letter yesterday afternoon from my sister who lives in Texas. 11. I did not write the letter; it is not mine. 12. He was walking behind me when we saw the man.

[15] The infinitive, instead of the present participle, is used after a preposition.

DIRECT AND INDIRECT OBJECTS

The use of direct and indirect object pronouns gives the beginner a great deal of trouble. The following suggestions should prove of great value in understanding and using them correctly.

The direct object (noun or pronoun) of a verb receives the action of the verb directly; that is, the direct object is acted upon by the subject. In the sentence: "John hits James," "James" is the direct object because he receives the action of the verb.

An indirect object is the person acted upon indirectly; that is, the person to or for whom the action of the verb is completed. Example: "John gives the ball to James." In this sentence the direct object is "ball," the thing acted upon, and "James" is the indirect object because "James" receives the action of the verb indirectly.

A good thumb rule for common practice: In a sentence in which there is an indirect object it is generally a person and receives something (the direct object) from the subject of the sentence. Test the following sentence:

"John throws the ball to Charles." The subject is "John" because he acts (throws) the direct object (ball) to the indirect object (Charles). Charles (the indirect object) receives the ball (the direct object) from John (the subject).

By substituting a pronoun for the direct and indirect object nouns in the above sentence, we have: "John throws it to him." "It" is the direct object pronoun, and "to him" is the indirect object pronoun (strictly speaking "to him" is a prepositional phrase in English).

Direct object pronouns		Indirect object pronouns	
Spanish	English	Spanish	English
me	me	me	to me
te	you (familiar)	te	to you (familiar)
le (m.)	you (formal)	le	to him
la (f.)	you (formal)	le	to her
le[16]	him	le	to you (formal)
la	her, it, you		
lo[16]	him, it		

[16] "Lo" on the Mexican border is often used as a direct object pronoun meaning "him," but "le" is considered better Spanish by most authorities.

Direct object pronouns		Indirect object pronouns	
Spanish	English	Spanish	English
nos	us	nos	to us
os	you (familiar)	os	to you (familiar)
los	you, them (m.)	les	to them (m. or f.)
las	you, them (f.)	les	to you (m. or f.)

A direct object is a noun or pronoun that receives the action of the verb directly. A direct object pronoun directly precedes the verb.

Él compró las plumas.	He bought the pens.
Él las compró.	He bought them.
Juan ve a María.	John sees Mary.
Juan la ve.	John sees her.
Yo tengo el libro.	I have the book.
Yo lo tengo.	I have it.
Ellos no nos vieron.	They did not see us.
Yo (le) ví a Juan.	I saw John.
Yo le (lo) ví.	I saw him.
¿Compró Vd. la casa?	Did you buy the house?
¿La compró Vd.?	Did you buy it?
Ella vendió sus plumas.	She sold her pens.
Ella las vendió.	She sold them.

If ambiguity exists when direct object pronouns of the third person are used, they may be further explained by the use of the prepositional pronoun.

La ví a ella anoche.	I saw her last night.
La ví a Vd. anoche. (f.)	I saw you last night.
Le ví a él anoche.	I saw him last night.
Le ví a Vd. anoche. (m.)	I saw you last night.

An indirect object receives the action of the verb indirectly.

Juan (le) dió la carta a Carlos.	John gave the letter to Charles.
Juan le dió la carta.	John gave the letter to him.
Le mandé diez dólares.	I sent her ten dollars.
Él le dijo la verdad.	He told you the truth.
Juan les vendió el carro.	John sold the car to them.

If ambiguity exists when the indirect object pronoun in the third person singular "le" (to you, to him, to her) or the third person plural "les" (to you, to them) is used, they may be explained further by the use of the prepositional pronoun.

Juan le dió la carta a ella.	John gave the letter to her.
Él le dijo la verdad a Vd.	He told you the truth.
Le mandé diez dólares a ella.	I sent her ten dollars.
Yo le doy el libro a él.	I give the book to him.
Él les da el libro a ellos.	He gives the book to them.
Él les da el libro a Vds.	He gives the book to you.

When a direct and an indirect object pronoun come together, the indirect always precedes the direct.

Carlos me lo dió.	Charles gave it to me.
María nos los vendió.	Mary sold them to us.
Juan me lo dijo.	John told it to me.
¿Nos las envió Vd.?	Did you send them to us?

When the direct and indirect object pronoun come together and both are in the third person singular or plural, the indirect precedes the direct and is written "se" instead of "le" or "les." This is done for euphony in order that two words beginning with "l" do not come together.

Se lo dí a él ayer.	I gave it to him yesterday.
¿No se lo dijo María a él?	Didn't Mary tell it to him?
Se lo llevé a él anoche.	I took it to him last night.
La madre de Juan se lo dió.	John's mother gave it to him.

In the first three sentences above it is necessary to further explain the use of "se" by the prepositional form, since "se" can have any one of several meanings. In the last sentence there is no ambiguity. Should the indirect object in this case be any other than "him," then it would be necessary to explain it further.

Se lo dí a él.	I gave it to him.
Se lo dí a ella.	I gave it to her.
Se lo dí a Vd.	I gave it to you.
Se lo dí a ellos. (m.)	I gave it to them.
Se lo dí a ellas. (f.)	I gave it to them.
Se lo dí a Vds. (pl.)	I gave it to you.
La mamá de Juan se lo dió.	John's mother gave it to him.
El padre de él se lo dió.	His father gave it to him.

In the last two sentences above there is really no necessity to further explain the use of "se" as the antecedent is perfectly clear. Should the indirect object have been other than as given, then the "se" would have needed further explanation.

The prepositional form may also be used with the first person singular or plural and second person singular or plural for emphasis.

María me lo dió a mí.	Mary gave it to me.
María te lo dió a ti.	Mary gave it to you.
María nos lo dió a nosotros.	Mary gave it to us.
María os lo dió a vosotros.	Mary gave it to you.

An indirect object noun is often anticipated by the use of the indirect object pronoun. Although the indirect object pronoun is not required, it is better Spanish to use it.

Le doy la pluma a Juan.	I give the pen to John.
Doy la pluma a Juan.	I give the pen to John.

Se la doy a Juan.	I give it to John.
La doy a Juan.	I give it to John.

Direct and indirect object pronouns follow the verb and are attached to the verb in the following forms:

1. Infinitive.[17]

Quiero dárselo a él.	I want to give it to him.
Él va a venderlos.	He is going to sell them.
Él quiere dárselo a ella.	He wants to give it to her.
Ellos quieren comprarlo.	They want to buy it.

2. Present Participle.[17]

Estoy escribiéndola ahora.	I am writing it now.
Él estaba hablándome.	He was talking to me.
Él está mostrándoselos (a ella).	He is showing them to her.
Ella está haciéndolo ahora.	She is making it now.

3. Affirmative command.

Enséñemelo Vd.	Show it to me.
Dígame Vd. la verdad.	Tell me the truth.
Escríbale Vd. a ella hoy.	Write to her today.
Véndame Vd. este libro.	Sell me this book.

In a negative command the object pronouns precede the verb.

No me lo dé Vd.	Do not give it to me.
No se lo enseñe Vd. a ellas.	Do not show it to them.

EXERCISE

1. Voy a venderlo mañana. 2. ¿En dónde lo compró Vd.? 3. ¿Por qué no se las mandó Vd. a él como le dije? 4. Yo quiero comprarla pero no tengo bastante dinero. 5. ¿Sabe Vd. por qué él no me lo dijo cuando (yo) le ví ayer? 6. ¿Cuándo la vió Vd. la última vez? 7. Él me lo dió el año pasado. 8. Voy a escribirle una carta. 9. Los compramos anteayer. 10. ¿Qué le dijo él a Vd. ayer? 11. Él no me dijo nada; no le ví. 12. Dígame Vd., ¿qué estaba haciendo cuando le ví anoche? 13. ¿Cuánto dinero le pagó María a Juana? 14. Juana me dijo que María le dió dos dólares. 15. Démelo Vd. 16. Tráigame Vd. una taza de café. 17. ¿En dónde lo puso Vd.?

---

[17] In the first and second cases above the object pronouns may completely precede the verb. However, it is suggested that the above forms be followed by the beginner.

EXERCISE

1. Why didn't you give it to him this morning? 2. How many dollars did he pay you? 3. Did Mary tell you the truth yesterday? 4. I want to buy it, but I do not have any money. 5. John is going to send it to me day after tomorrow. 6. Bring it to me now; I want to send it to John this afternoon. 7. Do you have your passport with you today? 8. No, sir, I lost it last week. 9. Do you know if your father sent it to me night before last? 10. Why don't you give it to me now? 11. Did he return it to you? 12. Did you write to her yesterday?

PRESENT INDICATIVE TENSE OF ALL IRREGULAR VERBS

Caber (to contain)

quepo	cabemos
cabes	cabéis
cabe	caben

Caer (to fall)

caigo	caemos
caes	caéis
cae	caen

Dar (to give)

doy	damos
das	dais
da	dan

Decir (to say, tell)

digo	decimos
dices	decís
dice	dicen

Estar (to be)

estoy	estamos
estás	estáis
está	están

Haber (to have (aux.))

he	hemos
has	habéis
ha	han

Hacer (to do, make)

hago	hacemos
haces	hacéis
hace	hacen

Ir (to go)

voy	vamos
vas	vais
va	van

Oír (to hear)

oigo	oímos
oyes	oís
oye	oyen

Poner (to put, place)

pongo	ponemos
pones	ponéis
pone	ponen

Saber (to know how)

sé	sabemos
sabes	sabéis
sabe	saben

Salir (to leave, go out)

salgo	salimos
sales	salís
sale	salen

Ser (to be)

soy	somos
eres	sois
es	son

Tener (to have, possess)

tengo	tenemos
tienes	tenéis
tiene	tienen

Traer (to bring)

traigo	traemos
traes	traéis
trae	traen

Valer (to be worth)

valgo	valemos
vales	valéis
vale	valen

Venir (to come)

vengo	venimos
vienes	venís
viene	vienen

Ver (to see)

veo	vemos
ves	veis
ve	ven

Although **"saber"** and **"conocer"** both mean "to know," they are not interchangeable. **"Saber"** means to know through having learned mentally. **"Conocer"** means to be acquainted with.

Yo sé la lección.	I know the lesson.
Él (le) conoce a mi papá.	He knows my father.

"Saber" means "to be able" or "know how" through having learned (a mental process). **"Poder"** means "to be able" in the sense of physically capable.

¿Sabe Vd. leer?	Do you know how to read?
	Can you read?
Él no puede leer.	He can't read. (Not physically able to do so.)
Él sabe escribir, pero no puede hoy porque se lastimó la mano ayer.	He knows how to write, but he cannot today because he hurt his hand yesterday.
Él sabe la lección.	He knows the lesson.
Él no puede ir.	He is unable to (can't) go.

VOCABULARY

la ofensa—the offense	**sin**—without
el federal—the officer	**bastante**—enough
una vez—once (one time)	**la pelota**—the ball
enseñar—to show, teach	**la vez**—the time
mandar—to order, send	**la taza**—the cup
el conocido—the acquaintance	**demasiado** (adj. or adv.)—too much
demasiados (adj.)—too many	**el delito**—the crime

EXERCISE

1. ¿Ha visto Vd. mi sombrero? 2. Sí, lo he puesto en la mesa. 3. Carlos conoce a mi amigo. 4. ¿No (le) conoce Vd. a este hombre? 5. Sí, señor, le he conocido (por) muchos años. 6. (Yo) No puedo ir esta tarde porque tengo que trabajar. 7. ¿Quiere Vd. regresar a México ahora? 8. Él está lejos y no puede oírme. 9. ¿Quién le trajo a Vd. a los Estados Unidos? 10. Un conocido mío me trajo.

EXERCISE

1. Do you have (any) friends in the United States? 2. I am going to Mexico in order to see my father. 3. Do you know how to read? 4. What time do they come to school? 5. They come to school at nine o'clock in the morning. 6. Why did you write this letter? 7. I wrote it because I wanted to see my son. 8. I do not know him. 9. I work for a man who talks Spanish. 10. Yes, I know it. 11. I have not seen the man. 12. Why do you wish to go to Texas?

THE PAST PERFECT INDICATIVE TENSES

PRETERITE PERFECT TENSE

In Spanish there are two past perfect tenses. The preterite perfect (formed by placing the preterite tense of the auxiliary verb **"haber"** before the past participle of the main verb) is very seldom used, and then only after such expressions as **"cuando," "luego que,"** etc. It is generally replaced by the simple preterite indicative.

Luego que hubo llegado él, fuimos al cine.	As soon as he had arrived, we went to the picture show.
Luego que él llegó, fuimos al cine.	As soon as he arrived, we went to the picture show.

Inasmuch as the preterite perfect is seldom used in Spanish and can always be replaced by the simple preterite, it is not treated further in this work.

PLUPERFECT INDICATIVE TENSE

The pluperfect (by some grammarians called the "past perfect") is formed by placing the imperfect tense of the auxiliary verb **"haber"** before the past participle of the main verb.

yo había comido	I had eaten
tú habías comido	you had eaten
él había comido	he had eaten
ella había comido	she had eaten
Vd. había comido	you had eaten
nosotros habíamos comido	we (masculine) had eaten
nosotras habíamos comido	we (feminine) had eaten
vosotros habíais comido	you (masculine) had eaten
vosotras habíais comido	you (feminine) had eaten
ellos habían comido	they (masculine) had eaten
ellas habían comido	they (feminine) had eaten
Vds. habían comido	you had eaten

IDIOMATIC USE OF "HUBO" AND "HABIA"

The third person singular of the imperfect indicative and the preterite indicative of the verb **"haber"** are used idiomatically to mean "there was" or "there were." Apply the rules for the use of the imperfect and preterite to determine which one to use.

Cuando yo era niño había mucha gente en la iglesia los domingos.
When I was a child there used to be many people in church on Sundays.
Ayer hubo mucha gente en la iglesia.
Yesterday there were many people in church.

VOCABULARY

el algodón—the cotton	**mostrar**—to show
el rancho—the ranch	**el marido**—the husband
el rancho—the farm	**la hacienda**—the farm
el campo—the country	**legalmente**—legally
el campo—the field	**la calle**—the street
el camino—the road	**la gente**—the people
mucha gente—many people	**el carro**—the car
el automóvil—the automobile	**el pueblo**—the town
había—there was, were	**el pueblo**—the people
hubo—there was, were	**la película**—the film, show
el cine—the picture show	

EXERCISE

1. Yo estaba trabajando (trabajaba) en un rancho cuando recibí la carta. 2. Él no había vivido en Arizona antes. 3. ¿Dijo él que iba a Tucsón? 4. No, señor, él dijo que iba a Las Cruces para comprar un automóvil nuevo. 5. Yo no le había visto a él antes. 6. ¿Por qué no me dijo Vd. la verdad? 7. Mi primo vive en la calle Elm. 8. Había mucha gente sin trabajo cuando salí de México. 9. Ella me dijo que había recibido muchas cartas de su esposo. 10. Entonces, es verdad que Vd. le pagó a él cinco dólares.

EXERCISE

1. I had bought the house when they arrived. 2. There was much (a lot of) cotton in the field. 3. He had gone to the office. 4. She did not come for the money because she had received a check. 5. Who lives with you now? 6. My aunt lives with me, but she was not at home when you came. 7. You told me that you had worked for him before. 8. I used to work for Mr. Jones, but now I am working on a ranch. 9. What did he tell you? 10. He said that he wanted to come to San Antonio.

THE POLITE COMMAND OF IRREGULAR VERBS

The polite command is obtained from the third person singular and plural of the present subjunctive. This topic was introduced on page 40, Lesson VII, but the irregular verbs were not treated in that lesson. At first glance many verbs will appear to be irregular. However, by attaching the proper endings ("e" and "en" for AR verbs and "a" and "an" for ER and IR verbs) to the stem of the first person singular of the present indicative tense, the polite command becomes regular in formation.

Infinitive		First person singular present indicative	Subjunctive-imperative	
English	Spanish		Singular	Plural
to have	tener	tengo	tenga Vd.	tengan Vds.
to do	hacer	hago	haga Vd.	hagan Vds.
to put	poner	pongo	ponga Vd.	pongan Vds.
to tell	decir	digo	diga Vd.	digan Vds.
to bring	traer	traigo	traiga Vd.	traigan Vds.
to come	venir	vengo	venga Vd.	vengan Vds.
to leave	salir	salgo	salga Vd.	salgan Vds.
to hear	oír	oigo	oiga Vd.	oigan Vds.
to see	ver	veo	vea Vd.	vean Vds.

The following verbs do not follow the above rule and should be memorized.

to be[18]	estar	estoy	esté Vd.	estén Vds.
to give[18]	dar	doy	dé Vd.	den Vds.
to go[19]	ir	voy	vaya Vd.	vayan Vds.
to be[19]	ser	soy	sea Vd.	sean Vds.
to know[19]	saber	sé	sepa Vd.	sepan Vds.

[18] These two verbs are irregular only in that they bear the written accent mark. "Estar" is conjugated like the same verb in the present tense except for the reversed endings. "Dar" has the written accent mark on the singular only to distinguish it from the preposition "de."

[19] These verbs are completely irregular.

SHORTENING OF ADJECTIVES

The following adjectives drop the final "o" when they precede a masculine singular noun:

bueno	good	un buen hombre	a good man
malo	bad	un mal muchacho	a bad boy
alguno	some	algún vino	some wine
ninguno	none	ningún café	no, not any coffee
uno	one	un caballero	one (a) gentleman
primero	first	el primer mes	the first month
tercero	third	el tercer día	the third day

"Grande" drops the last syllable "de" when it precedes a noun of either gender, and means "great" or "grand" rather than "large."

	un gran presidente	a great president
	una gran mujer	a great woman
	un gran hombre	a great man
but:	un hombre grande	a big man (size)
	una mujer grande	a large woman

"Ciento" drops the last syllable "to" when it precedes a noun of either gender.

	cien dólares	one hundred dollars
	cien sillas	one hundred chairs
	cien caballos	one hundred horses
but:	ciento quince caballos	one hundred fifteen horses
	dos cientas muchachas	two hundred girls

"Santo" drops the last syllable "to" when it precedes the masculine name of saints except those beginning with "Do" or "To."

San Pedro	St. Peter	Santa Ana	St. Anne
San Antonio	St. Anthony	Santa María	St. Mary
San Pablo	St. Paul	San Diego	St. James
Santo Domingo	St. Dominic	Santo Tomás	St. Thomas

THE RELATIVE PRONOUNS

The relative pronoun **"que"** meaning "that," "which," "who," or "whom" refers to persons or things. The relative pronoun **"quien"** meaning "who" or "whom" refers to persons only. **"Quien"** is used in place of **"que"** to introduce a nonrestrictive clause (one not necessary to complete the sentence).

La mujer que llegó es mi madre.	The woman who arrived is my mother.
Éste es el libro que él me dió (regaló).	This is the book that (which) he gave me.
Él le dió el libro a María, quien lo leyó con mucho gusto.	He gave the book to Mary, who read it with a great deal of pleasure.

| Él fué al pueblo con mi primo, quien pagó los gastos del viaje. | He went to town with my cousin, who paid the expenses of the trip. |

"Quien" often includes its antecedent, and is translated "he who," "the one who," etc.

| Quien[20] no estudia, no aprende. | He who doesn't study, doesn't learn. |
| Quienes[20] no tenían dinero, no fueron al cine. | Those who didn't have (any) money, did not go to the picture show. |

"Quien," and not **"que,"** relating to persons is used after a preposition.

| El hombre con quien fuí a la ciudad es mi tío. | The man with whom I went to town is my uncle. |
| ¿Para quién es este libro? | For whom is this book? |

"El que," "la que," etc., or **"el cual," "la cual,"** etc., may be used instead of **"que"** or **"quien"** (referring to persons or things) to avoid ambiguity when the relative pronoun is separated from its antecedent.

| Esta mañana le dí los libros que compré ayer, los que son muy interesantes. | This morning I gave him the books that I bought yesterday, which are very interesting. |
| Vamos a comprar las plumas a Juan, las que son de España. | We are going to buy the pens from John, which are from Spain. |

"Lo que" meaning "that which," "what" or "which" is used as a relative referring to an idea or fact rather than person or thing.

| No creo lo que él me dijo. | I do not believe what he told me. |
| Él prometió estudiar más, lo que agradó mucho a su papá. | He promised to study more, which (which fact) pleased his father very much. |

NEGATIVES

If a negative word is used after a verb, **"no"** must precede the verb. This is really a double negative and is not permissible in English. If the negative word comes before the verb, **"no"** is not required.

Nada tengo. ⎫ No tengo nada. ⎭	I have nothing. or, I do not have anything.
No veo a nadie.	I do not see anybody.
No tengo ningún libro.	I do not have a (any) book.
Ninguno de mis amigos está aquí.	None of my friends is here.
A!guien llama.	Someone is calling.
Nunca estudio. ⎫ No estudio nunca. ⎭	I never study.

[20] "Quien" and "quienes" in these examples may be replaced by "el que," and "los que" respectively.

VOCABULARY

nunca—never, ever
jamás—never, ever
siempre—always
unos—some, a few
nadie—no one, nobody
algo—something, anything
nada—nothing, not anything
ninguna cosa—nothing, not anything
también—also, too
tampoco—neither, either

ni . . . ni—neither . . . nor
ni—nor
todo el mundo—everybody
alguien—somebody, anybody
alguna cosa—something, anything
todo (adj. or pron.)—all, everything
alguno (adj. or pron.)—some, any
alguna vez—ever
ninguna (adj. or pron.)—none, not any
muchas veces—often

EXERCISE

1. Nunca he trabajado en los Estados Unidos. 2. Él no ha trabajado nunca en México. 3. Tampoco quiero ir: (or) no quiero ir tampoco. 4. ¿Tiene Vd. una pluma? No, señor.—¿Ni libros?—Tampoco. 5. Él no quiere hacerlo. Ni yo tampoco. 6. ¿Ha regresado Vd. alguna vez a México? 7. ¿Tiene Vd. (any[21]) dinero? 8. No tengo ni plumas ni lápices. 9. Él siempre llega a tiempo. 10. Todo el mundo necesita dinero. 11. Pagué cien dólares por el carro. 12. Él es un buen hombre pero no cree lo que le dije. 13. Nuestra vecina que vive en el campo es rica. 14. El verano pasado visitamos a nuestros abuelos quienes nos dieron mucho dinero. 15. La casa en que vivo es blanca pero no es tan bonita como la que vendí. 16. Venga Vd. a la oficina mañana a las nueve.

EXERCISE

1. Has your wife ever returned to Mexico? 2. No, she was born here and has always lived in the United States. 3. Do you always work on Sundays? 4. No, sir, sometimes I do not work on Sunday. 5. Do you have anything? I don't have anything. 6. Do you have any friends in the United States? 7. Some of my children live in the United States. 8. None of my friends knows that I am here. 9. He is a large man, but he is not a great man. 10. I paid him one hundred dollars on the first day of the third month. 11. My uncle is a good man. 12. I gave the money to my cousin who spent it for the car. 13. The man who bought my ranch is here. 14. This is the hat that I bought yesterday. 15. Bring me that book which is on the table. 16. Tell him that you don't know the man who gave you the money.

[21] "Any" is generally omitted in a sentence unless emphasis is desired.

COMPARISON OF ADJECTIVES

There are two ways of comparing adjectives in English:

Positive	Comparative	Superlative
slow	slower	slowest
beautiful	more beautiful	most beautiful

In Spanish the comparison of adjectives is formed by placing **"más"** before the positive for the comparative degree, and by placing the definite article before the comparative degree to obtain the superlative.

rico	(rich)	más rico	(richer)	el más rico	(richest)
rica	"	más rica	"	la más rica	"
ricos	"	más ricos	"	los más ricos	"
ricas	"	más ricas	"	las más ricas	"

"Than" is expressed by **"que"** in the comparative degree, and "of" by **"de"** in the superlative degree:

Soy más alto que María.	I am taller than Mary.
Ella es más rica que Juan.	She is richer than John.
Estas muchachas son más bonitas que aquéllas.	These girls are prettier than those.
Este hombre es el más rico del pueblo.	This man is the richest in town.
María es la más linda de la clase.	Mary is the prettiest of the class.
La mujer más alta no vino.	The tallest woman did not come.
La más alta mujer no vino.	The tallest woman did not come.

As seen in the last two examples above the word order of the superlative may take either form. The first is the more common.

The possessive adjective may take the place of the definite article:

Mi primo más alto está aquí.	My tallest cousin is here.
Su amigo más íntimo está malo.	His most intimate friend is sick.

In all of the examples on this page **"menos"** meaning "less" could have replaced **"más."**

There are four adjectives that are compared irregularly in Spanish:

Positive		Comparative		Superlative	
bueno	(good)	mejor	(better)	el mejor	(best)
malo	(bad)	peor	(worse)	el peor	(worst)
grande	(large)	mayor	(older)	el mayor	(oldest)
pequeño	(small)	menor	(younger)	el menor	(youngest)

"Grande" and "pequeño" are also compared regularly, in which case they have their regular meaning of size. The irregular comparison of "grande" and "pequeño" generally refers to "age."

Este hombre es mayor que mi hermano, y también es más grande.	This man is older than my brother, and also is larger.
Juan es el más pequeño de mis hijos, pero no es el menor.	John is the smallest (phys.) of my sons, but he is not the youngest.

Notice the following uses of "mayor" and "menor":

Perdí la mayor parte de mi dinero.	I lost the greater part (most) of my money.
Esta tienda vende al por mayor.	This store sells at wholesale.
Aquella tienda vende al por menor.	That store sells at retail.

ABSOLUTE SUPERLATIVE

The absolute superlative is formed by adding "ísimo, ísima, ísimos, or ísimas" to the adjective. If the adjective ends in a vowel, remove the vowel before attaching these endings. The absolute superlative does not directly compare one thing to another, but merely states "a great amount of," and can be translated in English by placing "very" before the adjective.

Adjective	Absolute superlative	English
linda	lindísima	very pretty
rico	riquísimo	very rich
mucho	muchísimo	very much
muchas	muchísimas	very many

The same idea can be expressed by using the adverb "muy" in front of the adjective; however, the absolute superlative is stronger. "Muy" cannot be properly used before "mucho, a," or "muchos, as."

María es lindísima.	Mary is very (extremely) pretty.
María es muy linda.	Mary is very pretty.
Muchísimas gracias.	Many, many thanks.
Hay muchísimas faltas en el ejercicio.	There are many errors in the exercise.
Esta sopa es muy rica.	This soup is very rich.

COMPARISON OF EQUALITY

In making comparisons of equality in Spanish, the English words "as," "as much," and "as many" are replaced by the Spanish words **"tan,"** **"tanto, a,"** **"tantos, as"** respectively. The second word "as" translated into Spanish by **"como"** is invariable.

tan . . . . **como**	as . . . . as
tanto, a . . . . **como**	as much . . . . as
tantos, as . . . . . . **como**	as many . . . . as

In the first case in the foregoing examples the comparison is of an adjective and the word **"tan"** is an adverb and is invariable. In the second and third cases above the comparisons are of amount and number of nouns, and the word stating the amount or number is an adjective and as such is variable as an adjective and agrees in number and gender with the word modified.

María es tan alta como Juan.	Mary is as tall as John.
Este libro es tan grande como el suyo.	This book is as large as yours.
Juan tiene tanto dinero como Eduardo.	John has as much money as Edward.
Hay tanta tinta en este tintero como en aquél.	There is as much ink in this inkwell as in that (one).
José tiene tantos libros como Ana.	Joseph has as many books as Anna.
Él ha escrito tantas cartas como Vd.	He has written as many letters as you.

"SINO"—HOW USED

The connective **"sino"** meaning "but" is used instead of **"pero"** in an affirmative statement in which the verb is omitted following a negative statement.

No voy al teatro sino a la iglesia.	I am not going to the theater but to church.
Él no es americano sino español.	He is not an American but a Spaniard.
but: **No tengo libros pero tengo plumas.**	I do not have any books, but I have some pens.

"ONLY"—HOW EXPRESSED

The English word "only" is expressed in several different ways in Spanish.

No leo sino libros ingleses.	I read only English books.
No tengo sino cuatro pesos.	I have only four dollars.
Tengo sólo cuatro pesos.	I have only four dollars.
Tengo cuatro pesos no más.	I have only four dollars. (I have four dollars no more.)

No tengo más que cuatro pesos.	I have only four dollars.
	(No more than four dollars.)
but: Tengo más de cuatro pesos.	I have more than four dollars.
Tengo menos de cuatro pesos.	I have less than four dollars.

VOCABULARY

tan—as	el metal—metal
tanto—as much, so much	duro—hard
tanta—as much, so much	durante—during
tantos—as many, so many	voluntariamente—voluntarily
tantas—as many, so many	limpio—clean
el teatro—the theater	el país—country
el huevo—egg	el pulgar—thumb
el blanquillo (in Mexico)—egg	la pulgada—inch
los muebles—the furniture	el dedo—finger
sucio—dirty	la cárcel—jail
íntimo—intimate	el minero—miner
sólo—only	la mina—mine
sino—but	mina de oro—gold mine
más . . . que—more . . . than	aunque—although
el pie—foot	acompañar—to accompany
a casa—to home (motion)	el ferrocarril—railroad
en casa—at home (location)	contento—contented
el vecino—neighbor	

EXERCISE

1. Él tiene tantos niños como el amigo de Vd. 2. Él no ha recibido tantas cartas de su esposa esta semana como la semana pasada. 3. ¿Cuándo salieron sus padres a México y cuántos muebles trajeron de allá? 4. No sé que trajeron porque yo no vine de aquel país con ellos. 5. Yo estuve allí tres semanas y entonces me dieron permiso para volver a casa. 6. Su amigo no es tan rico como Vd. pero está más contento. 7. ¿Cuánto oro sacó el minero de su mina durante el mes pasado? 8. Él me dijo que no había sacado tanto oro como el año pasado pero recibió más dinero por el oro porque el precio había subido. 9. Él me dijo que la mina era la mejor del Estado de Chihuahua pero que estaba muy lejos del ferrocarril. 10. El metal de oro no es muy duro pero vale mucho y pesa mucho. 11. Mi hermano mayor no ha visitado aquí desde el año mil novecientos treinta y cinco. 12. Yo no puedo pagarle (a Vd.) el dinero porque no tengo más que dos pesos y tengo que pagarle al médico. 13. ¿Quiere Vd. acompañarme al cine esta noche? Muchísimas gracias, señor, pero no puedo porque mi mamá está mala y tengo que quedarme en casa. 14. ¿Es buena la sopa? Sí, señor, es riquísima, pero está tan caliente que apenas puedo tomarla todavía. 15. El papá de María tiene una tienda y compra al por mayor y vende al por menor.

EXERCISE

1. Did you stay as long in Acapulco this year as last year? 2. No, I did not have as much money and returned home after two weeks. 3. Mr. Jones is the richest man in our town, but he is sick. 4. He lives in the tallest building on Tenth Avenue. 5. John does not earn more than five dollars a week, but he has more money in the bank than his brother because he does not spend as much. 6. He did not go to Colorado as the doctor told him, but to California because he had relatives there. 7. Although the car is old, he paid more than one thousand dollars for it. 8. I did not earn as much money last year as my brother, but he worked three months more than I. 9. I used to work ten hours every day when I lived in New York. 10. Mary is the prettiest girl in this town, but she does not have as many friends as Jane. 11. My grandparents did not bring many things from Mexico on account of (**a causa de**) the war. 12. My neighbors have worked very hard this year and have earned a great deal of (**mucho**) money. 13. Texas is larger than the State of New York, but there are more people in New York than in Texas.

THE NUMBERS

CARDINAL NUMBERS

cero	0	cincuenta	50
uno, a	1	cincuenta y uno	51
dos	2	cincuenta y dos	52
tres	3	sesenta	60
cuatro	4	sesenta y uno	61
cinco	5	sesenta y dos	62
seis	6	setenta	70
siete	7	setenta y uno	71
ocho	8	setenta y dos	72
nueve	9	ochenta	80
diez	10	ochenta y uno	81
once	11	ochenta y dos	82
doce	12	noventa	90
trece	13	noventa y uno	91
catorce	14	noventa y dos	92
quince	15	ciento (cien)	100
diez y seis	16	ciento uno	101
diez y siete	17	ciento dos	102
diez y ocho	18	doscientos, as	200
diez y nueve	19	trescientos, as	300
veinte	20	cuatrocientos, as	400
veinte y uno	21	quinientos, as	500
veinte y dos	22	seiscientos, as	600
veinte y tres	23	setecientos, as	700
treinta	30	ochocientos, as	800
treinta y uno	31	novecientos, as	900
treinta y dos	32	mil	1,000
cuarenta	40	dos mil	2,000
cuarenta y uno	41	tres mil	3,000
cuarenta y dos	42	un millón	1,000,000

The cardinal numbers, except **"uno"** and **"ciento,"** are invariable. These two numbers agree with the noun that they modify in gender and number. **"Ciento"** used alone before a masculine or feminine noun drops the final syllable (to) and becomes **"cien."** **"Uno"** drops the "o" when used before a masculine noun.

treinta libros	thirty books
treinta plumas	thirty pens

un libro	one book
una pluma	one pen
doscientos libros	two hundred books
doscientas plumas	two hundred pens
ciento un libros	one hundred and one books
ciento una plumas	one hundred and one pens
doscientos un libros	two hundred and one books
doscientos una plumas	two hundred and one pens
cien libros	one hundred books
cien plumas	one hundred pens

Starting with sixteen the compound numbers through twenty-nine in which **"y"** is used may be written as one word with a slight change in spelling:

diez y seis	dieciséis
diez y siete	diecisiete
veinte y uno	veintiuno
veinte y dos	veintidós

"Uno" is not used before **"ciento"** or **"mil"** unless needed to prevent ambiguity.

mil ciento ochenta y cinco	1,185
mil novecientos cuarenta	1,940

In forming the compound numbers the same word order is used in Spanish as in English. If the last number in a series is less than ten, **"y"** is used before the last number; otherwise **"y"** is not used. Most authorities do not use the conjunction **"y"** between hundreds and numbers under ten.

ciento diez	**110**
doscientos dos	**202**
ciento cuarenta	**140**

Counting above one thousand is not done by hundreds as is sometimes done in English.

mil ochocientos treinta	eighteen hundred and thirty
mil quinientos catorce	fifteen hundred and fourteen

In Spanish the word **"millón"** is a noun and is followed by the preposition **"de"** before the object enumerated.

dos millones de pesos	two million pesos
un millón de mujeres	one million women

ORDINAL NUMBERS

primero	1st
segundo	2nd

ORDINAL NUMBERS

tercero	3rd
cuarto	4th
quinto	5th
sexto	6th
séptimo	7th
octavo	8th
noveno	9th
décimo	10th

The ordinal numbers agree with the word they modify in gender and number. They are seldom used above tenth. **"Primero"** and **"tercero"** drop the "o" when used before a masculine singular noun.

la primera casa	the first house
el tercer hombre	the third man
la tercera calle	the third street
el tercer camino	the third road
la calle trece	Thirteenth Street
la quinta página	the fifth page
la página quince	page fifteen
los primeros libros	the first books
las primeras mujeres	the first women
Carlos sexto	Charles the Sixth
Carlos catorce	Charles the Fourteenth

The cardinal numbers are used with days of the month except the first.

El sábado es el primero de mayo.	Saturday is the first of May.
Nací el dos de mayo.	I was born the second of May.
El dieciséis de septiembre es día de fiesta en México.	The sixteenth of September is a holiday in Mexico.

VOCABULARY

el número—the number	nacer—to be born
el cumpleaños—the birthday	morir—to die
pensar—to think, intend	el recibo—the receipt
enterrar—to bury	sepultar—to bury
el sendero—the trail	quedarse—to remain, stay
permanecer—to remain, stay	estarse—to be, stay

EXERCISE

1. Mi papá vive en la calle Elm número 225. 2. Perdí el primer pasaporte que saqué. 3. Nací en México el dos de mayo de mil novecientos diez. 4. Mi hijo mayor nació el dos de enero de mil novecientos quince. 5. Hemos vivido dos años en la calle Oregon. 6. ¿En qué año nació Vd.? 7. Mi hija nació en mil ochocientos noventa y nueve. 8. ¿Es ésta la

primera vez que Vd. ha visitado a su tío? 9. Le visité dos veces el año pasado. 10. ¿Cuánto tiempo se quedó (permaneció) en México? 11. Pasé ocho días (una semana) en su casa antes de volver. 12. La primera casa que compré era blanca. 13. Él estaba en casa cuando llegué. 14. Cinco y seis son once. 15. El día primero (primer día) de marzo es mi cumpleaños. 16. Pasé más[22] de catorce días en Juárez.

EXERCISE

1. What is the number of the house in which you live? 2. The street on which I live does not have a name. 3. Does your father make much money? 4. My father earns very little, but my brother makes eighty-five dollars a (al) week. 5. I used to live in El Paso, but now I live one hundred miles from El Paso. 6. If you have so much money, why don't you buy a home? 7. I do not intend to stay here more than five days. 8. I paid eight dollars for this receipt. 9. His mother died in 1936. 10. This is the first day that I have worked here. 11. Do you intend to stay more than ten days in Mexico? 12. I lived ten years in Mexico before coming to the United States.

[22] "Than" before a number is "de" instead of "que."

THE FUTURE INDICATIVE TENSE

The future indicative tense of regular verbs is formed by adding the following endings to the whole infinitive for all three conjugations:

é, ás, á, emos, éis, án

Hablar

hablaré	I will or shall speak
hablarás	You will or shall speak
hablará	He will or shall speak
hablará	She will or shall speak
hablará	You will or shall speak
hablaremos	We will or shall speak
hablaréis	You will or shall speak
hablarán	They will or shall speak
hablarán	They will or shall speak
hablarán	You will or shall speak

Comer		Vivir	
comeré	comeremos	viviré	viviremos
comerás	comeréis	vivirás	viviréis
comerá	comerán	vivirá	vivirán

THE IRREGULAR VERBS OF THE FUTURE INDICATIVE TENSE

The twelve verbs listed below are the only irregular verbs of the future indicative tense. In five the vowel of the infinitive ending is deleted, and in five the vowel of the infinitive ending is changed to "d" before attaching the regular endings. In two, **"decir"** and **"hacer,"** the letters "ec" and "ce," respectively, are deleted from the infinitive.

Caber	—cabré	cabrás	cabrá	cabremos	cabréis	cabrán
Decir	—diré	dirás	dirá	diremos	diréis	dirán
Haber	—habré	habrás	habrá	habremos	habréis	habrán
Hacer	—haré	harás	hará	haremos	haréis	harán
Poder	—podré	podrás	podrá	podremos	podréis	podrán
Poner	—pondré	pondrás	pondrá	pondremos	pondréis	pondrán
Querer	—querré	querrás	querrá	querremos	querréis	querrán

Saber	—sabré	sabrás	sabrá	sabremos	sabréis	sabrán
Salir	—saldré	saldrás	saldrá	saldremos	saldréis	saldrán
Tener	—tendré	tendrás	tendrá	tendremos	tendréis	tendrán
Valer	—valdré	valdrás	valdrá	valdremos	valdréis	valdrán
Venir	—vendré	vendrás	vendrá	vendremos	vendréis	vendrán

THE FUTURE PERFECT TENSE

The future perfect is formed by placing the future indicative tense of the verb **"haber"** before the past participle of the main verb.

Hablar

habré hablado	I shall or will have spoken
habrás hablado	You shall or will have spoken
habrá hablado	He shall or will have spoken
habrá hablado	She shall or will have spoken
habrá hablado	You shall or will have spoken
habremos hablado	We shall or will have spoken
habréis hablado	You shall or will have spoken
habrán hablado	They shall or will have spoken
habrán hablado	They shall or will have spoken
habrán hablado	You shall or will have spoken

In addition to its regular use to express future time, the future tense may be used instead of the present indicative and the future perfect instead of the present perfect indicative to express probability or conjecture.

Juan no está aquí; estará malo.	John is not here; he is probably sick.
Él gasta mucho dinero; será rico.	He spends much money; he must be (is probably) rich.
Ella no tiene dinero ahora; se lo habrá dado a su hija.	She doesn't have any money now; she has probably given it to her daughter.

"Habrá" is used impersonally meaning "there will be" or "there shall be."

Creo que habrá mucha gente aquí mañana.	I think that there will be many people here tomorrow.

The present indicative tense of the verb **"ir"** preceding an infinitive is frequently used in Spanish to replace the future tense.

Voy a comer a las doce.	I am going to eat at twelve.
Comeré a las doce.	I shall eat at twelve.
Voy a estudiar esta noche.	I am going to study tonight.
Estudiaré esta noche.	I shall study tonight.

By comparing the above examples, it is readily seen that the English and Spanish usage of the future and the verb "to go" **(ir)** in the present indicative tense plus an infinitive express about the same idea.

VOCABULARY

plantar—to plant	**el campo**—the field
sentarse—to sit down	**la milpa**—the corn field
el hacendado—the farmer	**libertar**—to free, liberate.
el vaquero—the cowboy	**piscar**—to pick
el maíz—the corn	**la cosecha**—the harvest
la labor—the field	**renovar**—to renew
el jornalero—the laborer	**quedarse**—to remain
el albañil—the bricklayer	**la pereza**—laziness

EXERCISE

1. (Yo) Le daré la visa de inmigración a él. 2. Si le ve Vd. a él, dígale que yo vendré a su casa esta noche. 3. Siéntese Vd. en esta silla; volveré en un minuto. 4. ¿Estará Vd. en casa esta tarde a las seis? 5. No, tengo que ir a la oficina a esa hora pero volveré a las ocho. 6. Voy a Texas donde trabajaré en un rancho. 7. Los hacendados han plantado mucho maíz y habrá mucho trabajo. 8. Hay mucho algodón en las labores y quiero conseguir trabajo piscando algodón. 9. Hace seis meses que no tengo trabajo. 10. Fuí a México, en 1934 y me quedé allí más de dos años. 11. ¿Por qué no renovó Vd. su pasaporte? 12. Por la desidia no lo renové. 13. Vd. tendrá que ir a la oficina para sacar (conseguir) un permiso de visitante. 14. ¿Adónde irá Vd. después de la cosecha?

EXERCISE

1. Will you see the man tomorrow? 2. I will not see him tomorrow, but he will be here day after tomorrow. 3. At what time do you intend to leave? 4. I will leave at 7.30 A.M. 5. Will you tell him that I need some cowboys on my ranch? 6. If you have time, come back (return) this afternoon at six o'clock, and I will give you the paper. 7. Tell him that you will do it tomorrow. 8. Why don't you go to the office to talk to the inspector? 9. He will pay you tomorrow. 10. I will tell you everything that **(todo lo que)** he told me. 11. I have not seen them today, but I shall see them in the morning. 12. When do you intend to return to Colorado? 13. Go to the man's house and tell him that I will be there at eight o'clock. 14. Do you know the name of the man who came with you? 15. I do not know his name, but he was very tall.

THE CONDITIONAL TENSE

The conditional indicative tense (generally translated by would or should) is formed by adding the following endings to the infinitive for all three conjugations:

ía, ías, ía, íamos, íais, ían

Ir

iría	I would or should go
irías	You would or should go
iría	He would or should go
iría	She would or should go
iría	You would or should go
iríamos	We would or should go
iríais	You would or should go
irían	They would or should go
irían	They would or should go
irían	You would or should go

Dar—daría darías daría daríamos daríais darían.
Ver—vería verías vería veríamos veríais verían.

The endings for the conditional tense are always regular. The stem of verbs irregular in the conditional tense is the same as the stem of the future tense.

Haber—habré habrás habrá habremos habréis habrán. (Future.)
Haber—habría habrías habría habríamos habríais habrían. (Conditional.)

The conditional is sometimes used instead of the imperfect, and the conditional perfect instead of the pluperfect to express probability.

¿A qué hora llegó Vd.?	At what time did you arrive?
Serían las dos.	It was probably (about) two o'clock.
La mujer habría estado mala.	The woman had probably been sick.
Juan no vino a la escuela ayer; estaría enfermo.	John did not come to school yesterday; he was probably (must have been) ill.

THE CONDITIONAL PERFECT TENSE

The conditional perfect is formed by placing the conditional tense of the verb **"haber"** before the past participle of the main verb.

92

Ir

habría ido	I would or should have gone
habrías ido	You would or should have gone
habría ido	He would or should have gone
habría ido	She would or should have gone
habría ido	You would or should have gone
habríamos ido	We would or should have gone
habríais ido	You would or should have gone
habrían ido	They would or should have gone
habrían ido	They would or should have gone
habrían ido	You would or should have gone

VOCABULARY

viajar—to travel
dar empleo—to hire
ocupar—to hire
desocupar—to discharge
emplear—to employ
obtener—to obtain
prometer—to promise
desde—from, since
pararse—to stop, to stand up
hasta—until
entonces—then
al fin—at last
al fin de—at the end of
luego—then

el empleo—the employment
el cónsul—the consul
el correo—the mail
el correo—the post office
la estafeta—post office
la pistola—the pistol
el revólver—the revolver
platicar—to chat, talk
posible—possible
imposible—impossible
lo más pronto posible—as soon as possible
creer—to believe
dudar—to doubt

EXERCISE

1. ¿Qué querría Vd. hacer? Yo querría obtener permiso para visitar a mi hijo. 2. Él me dijo que iría mañana. 3. ¿Qué haría Vd. para aprender el español lo más pronto posible? 4. Yo leería muchos libros y entonces hablaría con la gente de habla española. 5. Yo viajaría por México y visitaría a mis amigos españoles. 6. ¿A qué hora cruzó Vd. la línea? Serían las once de la noche. 7. Ella me dijo que no vendría a los Estados Unidos sin su familia. 8. Él me escribió que no volvería a su trabajo hasta el once de mayo. 9. Vd. me prometió que le pagaría a él al fin del mes. 10. Él se paró pero no me dijo adonde iba. 11. Creo que Vd. podrá conseguir trabajo en los ranchos porque hay mucho algodón en las labores. 12. Dígame lo que estaba haciendo (hacía) Vd. ayer cuando llegamos a su casa. 13. ¿Entonces qué le dijo él a Vd.? Él me dijo que volvería a las seis de la tarde.

EXERCISE

1. He told me that he would return to this office at six o'clock. 2. Why

93

didn't you go to the office this morning to get a permit? 3. I did not go because the inspector told me that he would not be there. 4. I saw him and would have given him the money, but he did not stop. 5. Why didn't you tell me that before? 6. I did not think that you would believe me. 7. Nobody is at home; everybody has gone to town. 8. Didn't you answer the letter that you received from your wife? 9. I forgot to renew my passport. 10. Tell me what happened after the man arrived in the green car. 11. Did you pay him the money then?

THE REFLEXIVE

The verb is said to be reflexive when the subject and object are the same; that is, the subject does something to, or acts upon, itself. Many verbs that are not reflexive in English are so treated in Spanish. The reflexive pronouns follow the same rule for their location as do the direct and indirect object pronouns (page 67). In the infinitive form for vocabulary and dictionary research the reflexive verb is written with the third person reflexive pronoun attached.

PRESENT INDICATIVE TENSE

Levantarse — *To get oneself up*

Yo me levanto.	I get (myself) up.
Tú te levantas.	You get (yourself) up.
Él se levanta.	He gets (himself) up.
Ella se levanta.	She gets (herself) up.
Vd. se levanta.	You get (yourself) up.
Nosotros (as) nos levantamos.	We get (ourselves) up.
Vosotros (as) os levantáis.	You get (yourselves) up.
Ellos se levantan.	They (m) get (themselves) up.
Ellas se levantan.	They (f) get (themselves) up.
Vds. se levantan.	You get (yourselves) up.

Many verbs may be reflexive or not, according to whether the subject acts upon itself (reflexive) or upon something else (not reflexive).

Me lavo las manos.	I wash my hands. (reflexive)
Mi mamá me lava.	My mother washes me. (not reflexive)
Él se levantó temprano ayer.	He got up early yesterday. (reflexive)
Su mamá le levantó temprano ayer.	His mother got him up early yesterday. (not reflexive)

THE REFLEXIVE PRONOUNS AFTER PREPOSITIONS

mí—myself	nosotros, as—ourselves
ti—yourself	vosotros, as—yourselves
sí—himself	sí—themselves
sí—herself	sí—themselves
sí—yourself	sí—yourselves

Ella piensa siempre en sí.	She is always thinking of herself.
Él no habla nunca de sí.	He never speaks about himself.
No estamos pensando en nosotros.	We are not thinking about ourselves.

The above may be intensified by the use of **"mismo, a, os, as."**

Ella piensa siempre en sí misma.	She is always thinking of herself.
Él no habla nunca de sí mismo.	He never speaks about himself.
No estamos pensando de nosotros mismos.	We are not thinking about ourselves.
María misma me dijo.	Mary herself told me.
Yo mismo se lo dí a él.	I myself gave it to him.

The preposition **"con"** and the reflexive pronouns **"mi," "ti,"** and **"sí"** combine into **"conmigo," "contigo,"** and **"consigo,"** respectively.

¿Tiene Vd. su pasaporte consigo?	Do you have your passport with you? (yourself)
Nunca lo tiene consigo.	He never has it with him.

THE PASSIVE VOICE

There are two voices in Spanish as in English: The *active voice* in which the subject does the acting, and the *passive voice* in which the subject is acted upon by an agent.

The passive voice is formed in Spanish with the verb **"ser"** plus the past participle. The past participle in the Spanish passive agrees in number and gender with the subject of the verb. The agent is introduced by the preposition **"por"** if the action is physical, and by **"de"** if the action is mental.

El niño es amado de su mamá.	The child is loved by its mother.
Los niños son amados de sus padres.	The children are loved by their parents.
El hombre fué[23] arrestado por el policía.	The man was arrested by the policeman.
La muchacha fué castigada por su madre.	The girl was punished by her mother.
América fué descubierta por Colón.	America was discovered by Columbus.
La casa fué vendida ayer.	The house was sold yesterday.

It is not always necessary to express the agent as shown in the last example above.

THE RELEXIVE SUBSTITUTE FOR THE PASSIVE VOICE

In Spanish things and objects are considered as capable of acting upon

[23] In the passive voice in Spanish the verb "ser" is in the preterite tense in past time.

themselves, and the reflexive construction often replaces the English passive voice:

Aquí se habla español.	Spanish is spoken here. (Here Spanish speaks itself.)
Se venden libros en esta tienda.	Books are sold in this store. (Books sell themselves in this store.)
¿Cómo se dice eso en español?	How do you say that in Spanish? (How is that said in Spanish?)
En esta tienda se venden vestidos caros.	In this store expensive clothes are sold.
En esta tienda se venden vestidos caros a los ricos.	In this store expensive clothes are sold to the rich.
En esta tienda se les venden vestidos caros.	In this store expensive clothes are sold to them.

In the sentences just given the reflexive substitute is used instead of the passive voice. In the fourth sentence there is no indirect object expressed (to whom the clothes are sold). In the fifth sentence the indirect object is expressed by the noun **"ricos,"** and in the sixth sentence the indirect object noun **"ricos"** is replaced by the indirect object pronoun **"les."**

Se me olvidó el libro.	I forgot my book. (My book forgot itself to me.)
Se le perdió su pasaporte.	He lost his passport.
Se le prometió empleo.	He was promised employment.
Se me dió un sombrero.	A hat was given to me.
Se les envían periódicos.	Newspapers are sent to them.
Se me olvidaron las cartas.	I forgot the letters.

In the above examples the subject and verb agree with each other, and the reflexive **"se"** precedes all other object pronouns.

Olvidé mi pasaporte.	I forgot my passport.
Se me olvidó el pasaporte.	I forgot my passport.
Me olvidé el pasaporte.	I forgot my passport.

The last three sentences show different ways of expressing the same thought.

VOCABULARY

llamarse—to be named, to call (oneself)	**vestirse**—to dress (oneself)
sentarse—to seat oneself	**ponerse**—to put on (oneself)
levantarse—to get up	**quitarse**—to take off
lavarse—to wash (oneself)	**quedarse**—to remain, stay
acordarse de—to remember	**pararse**—to stop
acostarse—to go to bed	**pasearse**—to take a walk

97

1. ¿A qué hora se levantó Vd. esta mañana? 2. Me levanté a las seis esta mañana, pero estoy acostumbrado a levantarme poco más tarde. 3. ¿Cuánto tiempo se quedó Juan en Juárez antes de entrar en los Estados Unidos? 4. No me acuerdo de la fecha pero creo que él llegó allí el cinco del mes pasado. 5. Cuando entré en la casa anoche me quité el sombrero, me lavé la cara y las manos, y me senté a la mesa para comer. 6. María me dijo que ella no se lavó las manos porque no tenía tiempo. 7. ¿Cuántas veces se pararon Vds. en camino de Juárez a Las Vegas, y cuánto tiempo se quedaron en cada lugar? 8. Nos paramos cinco veces, pero no me acuerdo (de) que tanto tiempo nos quedamos en los varios (diferentes) lugares. 9. Enrique estaba lavándose cuando María le llamó por teléfono. 10. La muchacha es amada de su mamá porque es una muchacha buena. 11. Aquí se vende ropa al por mayor. 12. En este edificio se rentan cuartos y apartamientos a los pobres. 13. El padre es temido de su hijo porque (el padre) es un mal hombre. 14. Se me olvidaron los zapatos y tuve que comprar otro par. 15. El camino fué pavimentado por esa compañía en el año mil novecientos treinta.

1. What time did you go to bed last night? 2. It was about eleven thirty when I went to bed. 3. How long will it take you to dress yourself? (How long will you need in order to dress yourself?) 4. I put my hat on the table, but it is not there now. 5. How long did you stay in El Paso last year? 6. I remained here about four weeks before going to Tucson. 7. It was about eight o'clock when John left the house this morning. 8. I could not find my hat this morning although I knew that I had put it on the table last night. 9. Mary put on her coat and went to town. 10. I got up very early yesterday morning. 11. How long did you stay in that hotel before leaving for the United States? 12. He sat down beside me and began (empezó a) to talk to me about the war. 13. He washed his hands before going to the table. 14. The child's mother washes him every morning at nine o'clock. 15. Her mother got her up very early this morning. 16. Many books are sold in this store.

RADICAL CHANGING VERBS

There are three classes of radical changing verbs. The root vowel (the vowel of the syllable coming immediately before the infinitive ending) makes certain changes.

FIRST CLASSIFICATION

Radical changing verbs of the first classification include verbs of the first (ar) conjugation and the second (er) conjugation. The root vowel "o" changes to "ue" and "e" changes to "ie" when the stress falls on that syllable. This change takes place in nine places: 1st, 2nd, and 3rd persons singular, and 3rd person plural of the present indicative and of the present subjunctive and in the imperative singular.

FIRST CONJUGATION		SECOND CONJUGATION	
Pensar	**Contar**	**Perder**	**Volver**
Present indicative	*Present indicative*	*Present indicative*	*Present indicative*
pienso	cuento	pierdo	vuelvo
piensas	cuentas	pierdes	vuelves
piensa	cuenta	pierde	vuelve
pensamos	contamos	perdemos	volvamos
pensáis	contáis	perdéis	volváis
piensan	cuentan	pierden	vuelven
Present subjunctive	*Present subjunctive*	*Present subjunctive*	*Present subjunctive*
piense	cuente	pierda	vuelva
pienses	cuentes	pierdas	vuelvas
piense	cuente	pierda	vuelva
pensemos	contemos	perdamos	volvamos
penséis	contéis	perdáis	volváis
piensen	cuenten	pierdan	vuelvan
Imperative	*Imperative*	*Imperative*	*Imperative*
piensa	cuenta	pierde	vuelve
pensad	contad	perded	volved

99

SECOND CLASSIFICATION

Radical changing verbs of the second classification have verbs of the third (ir) conjugation. The root vowel "o" changes to "ue" and the root vowel "e" changes to "ie" in the same places as do radical changing verbs of the first classification. Verbs of this classification also change the "o" of the stem to "u" and the "e" of the stem to "i" when the terminal endings begin with "ie," "ió," or "a." These changes take place in the first and second persons plural of the present subjunctive, the third persons singular and plural of the preterite indicative, the present participle, and throughout the "ra" and "se" forms of the imperfect subjunctive.

WITH "o" IN THE STEM (Dormir)

Present indicative		Present subjunctive		Preterite indicative	
duermo	dormimos	duerma	durmamos	dormí	dormimos
duermes	dormís	duermas	durmáis	dormiste	dormisteis
duerme	duermen	duerma	duerman	durmió	durmieron

Imperfect subjunctive "ra" form		Imperfect subjunctive "se" form	
durmiera	durmiéramos	durmiese	durmiésemos
durmieras	durmierais	durmieses	durmieseis
durmiera	durmieran	durmiese	durmiesen

Imperative		Present participle
duerme	dormid	durmiendo

WITH "e" IN STEM (Sentir)

Present indicative		Present subjunctive		Preterite indicative	
siento	sentimos	sienta	sintamos	sentí	sentimos
sientes	sentís	sientas	sintáis	sentiste	sentisteis
siente	sienten	sienta	sientan	sintió	sintieron

Imperfect subjunctive "ra" form		Imperfect subjunctive "se" form	
sintiera	sintiéramos	sintiese	sintiésemos
sintieras	sintierais	sintieses	sintieseis
sintiera	sintieran	sintiese	sintiesen

Imperative		Present participle
siente	sentid	sintiendo

THIRD CLASSIFICATION

Radical changing verbs of the third classification have only verbs of the third (ir) conjugation, and in the root or stem the vowel is "e." This classification differs from the second classification in that the root vowel "e" changes to "i" when the stress is on the stem of the verb. When the terminal endings begin with "ie," "ió," or "a," the stem of the verb

100

changes "e" to "i" in the same manner as do radical changing verbs of the second classification.

WITH "E" IN THE STEM (Pedir)

Present indicative		Present subjunctive		Preterite indicative	
pido	pedimos	pida	pidamos	pedí	pedimos
pides	pedís	pidas	pidáis	pediste	pedisteis
pide	piden	pida	pidan	pidió	pidieron

Imperfect subjunctive "ra" form		Imperfect subjunctive "se" form	
pidiera	pidiéramos	pidiese	pidiésemos
pidieras	pidierais	pidieses	pidieseis
pidiera	pidieran	pidiese	pidiesen

Imperative		Present participle
pide	pedid	pidiendo

VOCABULARY

First classification

acordarse—to remember
acostarse—to go to bed
cerrar—to close
comenzar—to begin
confesar—to confess
costar—to cost
despertar—to awaken
devolver—to give back
encerrar—to enclose, lock up
encontrar—to meet, to encounter
empezar—to begin
entender—to understand
jugar—to play
llover—to rain
mostrar—to show
negar—to deny
nevar—to snow
poder—to be able
probar—to prove

querer—to wish, want
recordar—to remember

Second classification

consentir—to consent
divertirse—to amuse oneself
dormir—to sleep
mentir—to lie
morir—to die
preferir—to prefer
referir—to refer
sentir—to feel

Third classification

medir—to measure
pedir—to ask for
repetir—to repeat
seguir—to follow, continue
servir—to serve
vestirse—to get dressed

EXERCISE

1. Comienza a llover y por consiguiente no voy al teatro esta noche. 2. Él me dijo que no duerme bien cuando hace tanto calor. 3. No le entiendo a Vd. cuando habla tan de prisa. 4. Él se vistió y me siguió de su casa a la de mi tía. 5. Los sudamericanos no juegan tanto al béisbol (baseball) como nosotros los norteamericanos. 6. (Yo) Quiero que Vd. se vista y venga conmigo ahorita. 7. Despierto a las cinco y media todos

101

los días, pero no me levanto hasta las seis o las seis y cuarto. 8. Repita Vd. en voz alta y clara lo que me ha dicho. 9. (Yo) No puedo hacerlo porque tengo que ayudar a mi amigo Jorge. 10. ¿Cuánto cuestan las manzanas por docena? 11. El se divierte mucho cuando va a la ciudad. 12. (Yo) Confieso que (yo) no la sabía antes.

EXERCISE

1. How many hours do you sleep each night? 2. If you go to bed at ten P.M., you will be able to get up at six thirty A.M. 3. He does not understand me when I speak Spanish so fast. 4. They do not deny that she feels bad. 5. It rains almost every day during the summer and snows a great deal during the winter. 6. At what time do you begin your work? 7. Ask your father for a dollar, and we can go to the picture show; it costs only eighty cents for both of us. 8. Return (give back) his hat to him; he wants to put it on. 9. Close the door; I want to dress (myself). 10. He prefers to get up early because he cannot sleep well after six o'clock in the morning. 11. They followed us until we entered the store.

LESSON XXV

THE SUBJUNCTIVE MOOD

There are three moods in Spanish as well as in English: namely, the indicative, the subjunctive and the imperative.

The indicative mood points out a thing as material or existing either affirmatively or negatively and is based upon certainties or facts.

The imperative mood commands.

The subjunctive mood is subservient to, or contingent upon, some leading or governing idea expressed in an independent clause of causation, doubt, desire, emotion, or uncertainty. The subjunctive is a secondary or dependent thought or idea and is found in the dependent clause. The subjunctive never makes a direct statement nor asks a direct question.

THE PRESENT SUBJUNCTIVE

The present subjunctive is formed by attaching the following endings to the stem of the first person singular of the present indicative:

AR verbs: e, es, e, emos, éis, en
ER verbs: a, as, a, amos, áis, an
IR verbs: a, as, a, amos, áis, an

Hablar	Comer	Escribir
habl–e	com–a	escrib–a
habl–es	com–as	escrib–as
habl–e	com–a	escrib–a
habl–emos	com–amos	escrib–amos
habl–éis	com–áis	escrib–áis
habl–en	com–an	escrib–an

Note: The endings of the present subjunctive of verbs are the reverse of the present indicative; that is, "ar" verbs are conjugated like "er" verbs, and "er" and "ir" verbs are conjugated like "ar" verbs with the exception of the first person singular, which is the same as the third person singular.

The following verbs do not follow the above rule for the formation of the present subjunctive and must be memorized as irregular verbs:

haber—haya	hayas	haya	hayamos	hayáis	hayan
ir—vaya	vayas	vaya	vayamos	vayáis	vayan
saber—sepa	sepas	sepa	sepamos	sepáis	sepan
ser—sea	seas	sea	seamos	seáis	sean

THE PRESENT PERFECT SUBJUNCTIVE

The present perfect subjunctive is formed by placing the present subjunctive of the auxiliary verb **"haber"** in front of the past participle of the principal verb.

Tomar	Vender	Escribir
haya tomado	haya vendido	haya escrito
hayas tomado	hayas vendido	hayas escrito
haya tomado	haya vendido	haya escrito
hayamos tomado	hayamos vendido	hayamos escrito
hayáis tomado	hayáis vendido	hayáis escrito
hayan tomado	hayan vendido	hayan escrito

THE IMPERFECT SUBJUNCTIVE

The imperfect subjunctive has two forms called the first, or "ra" form, and the second, or "se" form. The imperfect subjunctive is formed by adding the following endings to the stem of the 3rd person plural of the preterite indicative.

The first or "ra" form

AR verbs:	ara	aras	ara	áramos	arais	aran
ER verbs:	iera	ieras	iera	iéramos	ierais	ieran
IR verbs:	iera	ieras	iera	iéramos	ierais	ieran

Tomar	Vender	Escribir
tom–ara	vend–iera	escrib–iera
tom–aras	vend–ieras	escrib–ieras
tom–ara	vend–iera	escrib–iera
tom–áramos	vend–iéramos	escrib–iéramos
tom–arais	vend–ierais	escrib–ierais
tom–aran	vend–ieran	escrib–ieran

The second or "se" form

AR verbs:	ase	ases	ase	ásemos	aseis	asen
ER verbs:	iese	ieses	iese	iésemos	ieseis	iesen
IR verbs:	iese	ieses	iese	iésemos	ieseis	iesen

Tomar	Vender	Escribir
tom–ase	vend–iese	escrib–iese
tom–ases	vend–ieses	escrib–ieses
tom–ase	vend–iese	escrib–iese
tom–ásemos	vend–iésemos	escrib–iésemos
tom–aseis	vend–ieseis	escrib–ieseis
tom–asen	vend–iesen	escrib–iesen

Those verbs whose stem ends in a "j" in the preterite indicative drop the "i" of the imperfect subjunctive throughout:

| Decir: | dij–era | dijeras | dijera | etc. |
| | dij–ese | dijeses | dijese | etc. |

An unaccented "i" between vowels becomes "y" in Spanish:

| Leer: | le–yera | leyeras | leyera | etc. |
| | le–yese | leyeses | leyese | etc. |

THE PLUPERFECT SUBJUNCTIVE

The pluperfect subjunctive is formed by placing the imperfect subjunctive of the verb "haber" in front of the past participle of the main verb.

The first or "ra" form

Tomar	Comer	Vivir
hubiera tomado	hubiera comido	hubiera vivido
hubieras tomado	hubieras comido	hubieras vivido
hubiera tomado	hubiera comido	hubiera vivido
hubiéramos tomado	hubiéramos comido	hubiéramos vivido
hubierais tomado	hubierais comido	hubierais vivido
hubieran tomado	hubieran comido	hubieran vivido

The second or "se" form

Tomar	Comer	Vivir
hubiese tomado	hubiese comido	hubiese vivido
hubieses tomado	hubieses comido	hubieses vivido
hubiese tomado	hubiese comido	hubiese vivido
hubiésemos tomado	hubiésemos comido	hubiésemos vivido
hubieseis tomado	hubieseis comido	hubieseis vivido
hubiesen tomado	hubiesen comido	hubiesen vivido

THE FUTURE SUBJUNCTIVE AND FUTURE PERFECT SUBJUNCTIVE

The future subjunctive and the future perfect subjunctive are seldom used; therefore, they have been omitted from this course.

USES OF THE SUBJUNCTIVE

AFTER VERBS OF CAUSING

If the verb of the independent (main) clause is one that causes another person or thing to act or not to act, the verb of the dependent clause will be in the subjunctive. The following verbs in the independent clause require the verb of the dependent clause to be in the subjunctive provided there is a change of subject in the clauses:

mandar—to order	preferir—to prefer
mandar—to command	prohibir—to prohibit
decir—to tell (order)	rogar—to beg, pray
impedir—to impede	pedir—to ask for
permitir—to permit	proponer—to propose

(Yo) Mando que Vd. vaya.	I order you to go. (I order that you go.)
Él me dijo que volviera.	He told me to return. (He told me that I return.)
El inspector no permitirá que yo vaya.	The inspector will not permit me to go. (The inspector will not permit that I go.)
Preferimos que Vd. saque (obtenga) (un) pasaporte.	We prefer that you take out (obtain) a passport.
El oficial prohibió que yo entrara.	The officer prohibited me to enter (my entering).
Le ruego que Vd. no haga por mí.	I beg you to do it for me. (I beg that you do it for me.)
Él me pidió que (yo) volviera a las seis.	He asked me to return at six. (He asked that I return at six.)
Él impidió que María volviera (regresara).	He prevented Mary's returning. (He prevented that Mary return.)
Prefiero ir.	I prefer to go. (No change of subject.)

For the above example, and all following ones, see "Sequence of Tenses" (page 111) for the method of determining the proper tense of the subjunctive clause.

EXPRESSIONS OF FEELING OR EMOTION

If the verb of the main clause expresses emotion or feeling, the verb of the dependent clause will be in the subjunctive.

extrañarse—to be surprised	tener miedo—to be afraid
alegrarse de—to be glad	sentir—to be sorry
esperar—to hope (expect)	temer—to fear

Espero que Carlos llegue a tiempo.	I hope that Charles arrives on time.
Nos alegramos de que Vds. no estuvieran malos.	We are glad that you were not sick.
Él extrañó que (yo) no hubiera trabajado más.	He was surprised that I had not worked more.
Siento que él haya estado malo.	I am sorry that he has been sick.
Espero ir.	I hope to go. (No change of subject; therefore, no subjunctive.)

EXPRESSIONS OF DOUBT OR DENIAL

If the verb of the main clause expresses doubt or denial or is used nega-

106

tively or interrogatively expressing belief or understanding, the verb of the dependent clause will be in the subjunctive.

dudar—to doubt.	no creer—not to believe
negar—to deny	no imaginarse—not to imagine
creer—to believe	no figurarse—not to believe

Él duda que yo tenga tanto dinero.	He doubts that I have so much money.
María no cree que Juan estuviera malo.	Mary does not believe (think) that John was sick.
Ella niega que yo le diera el dinero.	She denies that I gave her the money.
¿Se figura Vd. que sus padres hayan llegado?	Do you think that your parents have arrived?
No puedo figurarme que Juan lo hiciera.	I cannot imagine (figure) that John did it.
No dudo que él está malo.	I don't doubt that he is sick. (Indicative, as no doubt expressed.)
Enrique no niega que él lo hizo.	Henry does not deny that he did it. (No denial; therefore, the indicative.)

IMPERSONAL EXPRESSIONS

The subjunctive is used after impersonal expressions unless certainties are expressed.

es preciso—it is necessary	es justo—it is just
es necesario—it is necessary	es lástima—it is a pity
es posible—it is possible	es dudoso—it is doubtful
es injusto—it is wrong	es importante—it is important

Es posible que él no tenga dinero.	It is possible that he does not have (any) money.
Es lástima que Guillermo no se sienta mejor.	It is a pity that William does not feel better.
Es preciso que Vd. venga conmigo.	It is necessary that you come with me.
Es dudoso que él llegue a tiempo.	It is doubtful that he will arrive on time.
Importa que Vd. estudie cada día.	It is important that you study each day.
Es cierto que él no llegó a tiempo.	It is certain that he did not arrive on time. (No doubt or uncertainty.)

AFTER RELATIVE PRONOUNS

The subjunctive is used in the dependent clause after a relative pronoun referring to a person or thing that is indefinite or unknown.

107

Busco una criada que sepa cocinar.	I am looking for a servant (unknown to the speaker) who knows how to cook.
Daré dos pesos al muchacho que me enseñe la casa.	I'll give two pesos to the boy (unknown) who shows me the house.
Dí dos pesos al muchacho que me enseñó la casa.	I gave two pesos to the boy (now known) who showed me the house.

AFTER CONJUNCTIVE EXPRESSIONS

The subjunctive is used after certain adverbial conjunctions when they express indefinite future time, supposition, purpose, result, concession, or provision. Where there is no doubt or uncertainty in the mind of the speaker or an indefinite future time is not expressed, the indicative and not the subjunctive mood is used.

suponiendo que—supposing that
con tal (de) que—provided that
en caso (de) que—in case that
siempre que—provided that
en cuanto—as far as (when)
de manera que—in order that
antes de que—before
para que—in order that
luego que—as soon as

para cuando—by the time when
a pesar de que—in spite of
dado que—granted that
mientras que—while
a menos que—unless
hasta que—until
aunque—although
tal que—such that
cuando—when

Yo esperaré hasta que Vd. venga.	I shall wait until you come.
Él irá mañana a menos que haga mal tiempo.	He will go tomorrow unless the weather is bad.
Le permitirán entrar con tal que tenga pasaporte local.	They will permit you to enter provided you have a passport.
Luego que él obtenga (saque) una visa de inmigración, vendrá a los Estados Unidos.	As soon as he obtains (takes out) an immigration visa, he will come to the United States.
Yo esperé hasta que él llegó.	I waited until he arrived. (not indefinite, therefore, the indicative and not the subjunctive.)

IN CONDITIONS CONTRARY TO FACT

Conditions Contrary to Fact in Present Time.

The verb in the "result clause" will be in the conditional, and the verb in the "if clause" will be in the imperfect subjunctive. The word order of these two clauses does not matter; either may come first. In the following examples, the "result clause" is underlined in both English and Spanish.

I would buy the house if I had the money.
Yo compraría la casa si tuviera (el) dinero.
Si tuviera (el) dinero, yo compraría la casa.

If there were plenty of work in Mexico, would you be there?
¿Si hubiera bastante trabajo en México, estaría Vd. allí?
¿Estaría Vd. allí si hubiera bastante trabajo en México?

Would you tell him the truth if he were here?
¿Le diría la verdad si él estuviera aquí?
¿Si él estuviera aquí, le diría (Vd.) la verdad?

If you did not have employment, I would help you.
Si Vd. no tuviera empleo, le ayudaría a Vd.
Le ayudaría a Vd. si (Vd.) no tuviera empleo.

I would go to town if it were not so warm.
Iría al pueblo si no hiciera tanto calor.
Si no hiciera tanto calor, iría al pueblo.

Would you return to Mexico if you had the opportunity?
¿Regresaría Vd. a México si tuviera la oportunidad?
¿Si tuviera la oportunidad, regresaría Vd. a México?

Notice the first example: "I would buy the house if I had the money."
I do not have the money; therefore, the condition is contrary to fact.

In the "if clause" either the "ra" or "se" form of the imperfect subjunctive may be used, and in the "result clause" either the conditional or the "ra" form of the imperfect subjunctive may be used. However, until the student becomes quite familiar with the subjunctive, it is suggested that the forms given in these examples be used.

Conditions Contrary to Fact in Past Time.

The verb of the "result clause" will be in the conditional perfect and the verb of the "if clause" will be in the pluperfect subjunctive. It does not matter which of these two clauses precedes. The "result clause" is underlined in both Spanish and English.

I would have bought the house if I had had the money.
Yo habría comprado la casa si hubiera tenido el dinero.
Si hubiera tenido (el) dinero, yo habría comprado la casa.

If there had been plenty of work in Mexico, would you have come to the United States?
¿Si hubiera habido bastante trabajo en México, habría venido Vd. a los Estados Unidos?
¿Habría venido Vd. a los Estados Unidos si hubiera habido bastante trabajo en México?

Would you have told him the truth if he had been here?
¿Le habría dicho la verdad si él hubiera estado aquí?
¿Si él hubiera estado aquí, le habría dicho Vd. la verdad?

109

If you had not had employment, I would have helped you.
Si Vd. no hubiera tenido empleo, (yo) le habría ayudado.
(Yo) Le habría ayudado si Vd. no hubiera tenido empleo.

I would have gone to town if it had not been so warm.
Habría ido al pueblo si no hubiera hecho tanto calor.
Si no hubiera hecho tanto calor, yo habría ido al pueblo.

Would you have returned to Mexico if you had had the opportunity?
¿Habría regresado (vuelto) a México si Vd. hubiera tenido la oportunidad?
¿Si Vd. hubiera tenido la oportunidad, habría regresado (vuelto) a México?

I would have remained in Mexico if I had been you.
Yo me habría quedado en México si hubiera sido Vd.

IN THE IMPERATIVE

The subjunctive has a special use in giving direct commands. This is often called the polite or formal imperative and requires that Vd. or Vds. be the person addressed.

Vaya Vd. a la oficina y dígale al inspector que quiere visitar a su tío.	Go to the office and tell the inspector that you wish to visit your uncle.
Firme (escriba Vd. su nombre) con tinta en esta línea (raya).	Sign (write) your name in ink on this line.
Véngase Vd. por acá, quiero hablarle.	Come here, I wish to talk to you.
Déme Vd. esa camisa.	Give me that shirt.
Enséñeme Vd. su pasaporte.	Show me your passport.
Déjeme ver esa carta que Vd. tiene en el bolsillo.	Let me see that letter that you have in your pocket.
Escriba Vd. a su papá y dígale que Vd. no tiene bastante dinero.	Write to your father and tell him that you do not have enough money.
Afloje Vd. la mano.	Relax your hand.
Vaya Vd. a casa.	Go home.
Cierre Vd. la puerta antes de salir.	Close the door before leaving (going out).
Siéntese Vd. en esta silla.	Sit down in this chair.

There are several ways in which a polite command or mild wish or desire may be expressed in Spanish.

Quisiera ir a México este año.	I should like to go to Mexico this year.
Quisiera comprar aquella casa.	I should like to buy that house.
Desearía vender mi carro.	I should like to sell my car.
Me gustaría comer allí esta noche.	I should like to eat there tonight.
Querría que Vd. viniera conmigo.	I should like you to come with me.
Quisiera que Vd. no lo hiciera.	I should like you not to do it.

110

Desearía que Vd. me escribiera más a menudo.	I should like you to write me more often.
Me gustaría que Vd. me diera el documento.	I should like you to give me the document.

The subjunctive is used after **"ojalá"** (that God grant) which has the force of a verb of wishing.

Ojalá que recibamos la carta hoy.	I wish that (O that) we receive the letter today.
Ojalá que venga él mañana.	I wish that he would come tomorrow.
Ojalá que mi primo estuviera aquí.	O that (I wish that) my cousin were here.
Ojalá que Juan tuviera el dinero.	O that John had the money.
Ojalá que (yo) hubiera ahorrado más dinero.	O that I had saved more money.

SEQUENCE OF TENSES

The chart on page 112 shows the time relation in Spanish of the tense of the subjunctive in the dependent clause to that of the indicative in the independent clause.

Generally speaking, the tense of the independent and the dependent (subjunctive) clauses will be the same in Spanish as in English.

If the verb of the independent clause is in the primary (present, present perfect, or future) and the action of the dependent (subjunctive) took place before the verb of the independent clause, the verb of the dependent (subjunctive) clause will be in the imperfect subjunctive or the present perfect subjunctive. If the action was in a definite past time and in no way connected with the present or present perfect time, the imperfect subjunctive will be used. If the action is in any way connected with the present time, the present perfect subjunctive will be employed.

Temo que él estuviera malo la semana pasada.	I am afraid that he was sick last week.
Dudo que él perdiera el dinero como dijo.	I doubt that he lost the money as he said.
No creo que él le dijera la verdad ayer.	I do not believe that he told you the truth yesterday.
Temo que él haya estado malo esta semana.	I am afraid that he has been sick this week.
Dudo que él haya perdido tanto dinero como Juan este año.	I doubt that he has lost as much money as John this year.
Me extraño que él no haya llegado todavía.	I am surprised that he has not arrived yet.

In the above examples, the first three were definitely past actions in the dependent clause as far as the independent clause was concerned.

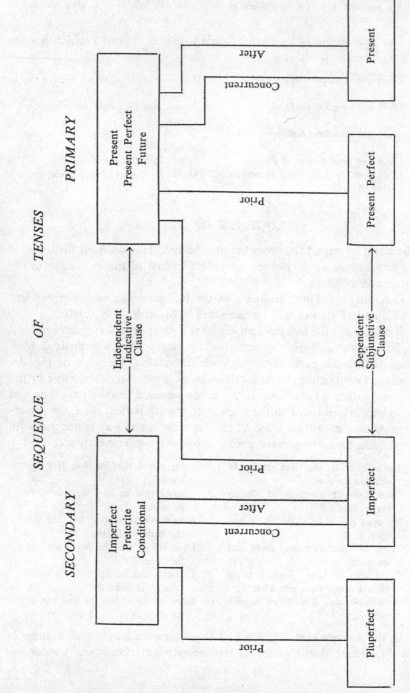

SEQUENCE OF TENSES

PRIMARY

| Present |
| Present Perfect |
| Future |

After — Present
Concurrent — Present

Prior — Present Perfect

Independent Indicative Clause

Dependent Subjunctive Clause

Prior — Imperfect

SECONDARY

| Imperfect |
| Preterite |
| Conditional |

After — Imperfect
Concurrent — Imperfect

Prior — Pluperfect

There was no connection with the present time; therefore, the imperfect subjunctive was used. In the last three examples, the dependent verb action, although past, is connected with the verb of the independent clause in that the action was completed within the same period of time.

If the action of the verb of the dependent clause takes place at the same time or later than the action of the independent clause, the verb of the dependent clause will be in the present subjunctive.

Siento mucho que Juan esté malo.	I am sorry that John is sick.
María duda que Carlos gane tanto dinero.	Mary doubts that Charles earns that much money.
No creo que él esté aquí hoy.	I do not think that he is here today.
Temo que él no escriba la carta mañana.	I fear that he won't write the letter tomorrow.
Esta tarde le diré a él que venga a la oficina mañana.	This afternoon I shall tell him to come to the office tomorrow.

If the verb of the independent clause is in the secondary (imperfect, preterite, conditional) and the action of the dependent clause precedes, then the dependent clause will be put in the pluperfect subjunctive.

Yo dudé que él hubiera vivido en los Estados Unidos, alguna vez.	I doubted that he had ever lived in the United States.
Mi amigo sentía mucho que yo hubiera perdido el dinero.	My friend was very sorry that I had lost the money.
María temía que su mamá hubiera estado mala.	Mary was afraid that her mother had been ill.
Él no creyó que ella hubiera dicho la verdad.	He did not believe that she had told the truth.

If the verb of the dependent clause has its action at the same time or later than the verb in the independent clause, it is put in the imperfect subjunctive.

Yo dudé que él estuviera en Los Ángeles.	I doubted that he was in Los Angeles.
Él me mandó que (yo) volviera al día siguiente.	He ordered me to return the following day.
Él no creía que (yo) estuviera malo.	He did not believe that I was sick. (same time)
Le pedí que me escribiera.	I asked him to write me.
Ella le dijo que volviera.	She told him to return.
Mandaron que yo fuera.	They ordered me to go.

If a pronoun is the subject of the dependent verb after an impersonal expression or after a verb of causation, the object pronoun may be used with the infinitive instead of the subjunctive.

Yo le dejo entrar.	I let (allow) him to enter.
Yo le dejo que entre.	I let (allow) him to enter.
Él me prohibió entrar.	He prohibited my entering.

Él prohibió que yo entrara.	He prohibited my (me from) entering.
Mi padre me hizo estudiar.	My father made me study.
Mi padre me hizo que estudiara.	My father made me study.
Me es imposible hacerlo.	It is impossible for me to do it.
Es imposible que yo lo haga.	It is impossible for me to do it.

The infinitive is not used after **"querer," "pedir," "rogar,"** and **"decir."**

Él quiere que yo vaya.	He wants me to go.
El inspector me dijo que volviera.	The inspector told me to return.
Le rogué que lo hiciera.	I asked him to do it.

If a noun is the subject of the dependent verb, the subjunctive is required.

Prohibí que Juan entrara.	I prevented John's entering.
Él mandó que Juan volviera a las seis.	He ordered John to return at six o'clock.

LESSON XXVI

SPECIAL USE OF SOME VERBS

In English there is a difference between a gerund and a present participle; however, for our purposes no distinction need be made and all forms of the verb ending in "ing" are called present participles.

An infinitive preceded by the definite article **"el"** is used as a verbal noun and is translated by the present participle in English.

El estudiar es importante.	Studying is important.
El nadar es buen ejercicio.	Swimming is good exercise.

An infinitive is used instead of a present participle after a preposition.

Después de ir a la oficina, hablamos al inspector.	After going to the office, we talked to the inspector.
Él salió sin verme.	He left without seeing me.

"On" followed by a present participle in English is translated by **"al"** followed by the infinitive in Spanish.

Al llegar a casa, ví a mi hermana.	On arriving home, I saw my sister.
Al salir del cine, le encontré en la calle.	On coming out of the picture show, I met him on the street.

In the use of **"gustar"** meaning "to like" or "to please" the English subject becomes the object and the English object becomes the subject in Spanish:

Me gusta el libro.	I like the book. (The book pleases me.)
Les gusta nadar.	They like to swim.
¿Le gustan a Vd. las manzanas?	Do you like apples?

Notice that the subject generally follows the verb although it may precede.

Likewise **"faltar"** and **"hacer falta"** meaning "to want" or "to need" are used by changing the English subject to the Spanish object and the English object to the Spanish subject.

Me faltan (hacen falta) cinco libros más.	I need five more books. (Five more books are lacking to me.)
Nos faltaba el dinero para hacer el viaje.	We lacked (needed) the money for making the trip.

"Hacer" may be used to cause a person to do something or cause something to be done.

Mi padre me hace estudiar.	My father makes me study.
Él hizo construir una casa grande.	He had a large house made.

"Tener que" plus an infinitive meaning "to have to" expresses compulsion or absolute necessity.

Vd. tiene que obtener permiso antes de visitar a su madre.	You have to obtain permission before visiting your mother.
Él tendrá que volver dentro de seis días.	He will have to return within six days.

"Hay que" plus an infinitive is used impersonally to express necessity.

Hay que estudiar mucho para aprender el español.	It is necessary to (one must) study a great deal in order to learn Spanish.
Hay que trabajar mucho para ganar la vida.	One must work hard to earn a living.

About the same meaning would be obtained by the use of **"es necesario"** or **"es preciso"** followed by the infinitive.

Es necesario trabajar mucho para ganar la vida.	It is necessary to work hard in order to make a living.
Es preciso hacerlo.	It is necessary to do so (it).

"Haber de" plus an infinitive expresses a mild obligation.

He de jugar a la pelota esta tarde.	I am to play ball this afternoon.
Ellos han de llegar a las tres.	They are to arrive at three o'clock.

"Deber (de)" plus an infinitive expresses obligation or duty, but not compulsion or force.

Debo estudiar mi lección.	I ought to study my lesson. (I must study my lesson.)
Vd. debe de ir a casa.	You ought to go home.
Vd. debería (debiera) planchar la camisa antes de ponérsela.	You ought to (should) iron the shirt before putting it on.
Vd. debiera haber planchado la camisa.	You ought to have ironed the shirt.

VOCABULARY

importante—important	cobrar—to collect
nadar—to swim	montar a caballo—to ride horseback
la cuenta—the bill	escaparse—to escape
el saco—the coat	el baile—the dance
el ladrillo—the brick	el negocio—the business
de seda—of silk	perezoso—lazy

la manzana—the apple
el viaje—the trip
ponerse—to put on
planchar—to iron
la camisa—the shirt
construir—to construct
la llanta—the tire

por eso—on that account, for that reason
la salud—the health
la plaza—the square (plaza)
demasiado—too much
quitarse—to take off

EXERCISE

1. Vd. no debe irse sin pagar la cuenta. 2. Un ranchero prometió darme empleo (trabajo); por eso, decidí venir a los Estados Unidos. 3. Después de pagarle cinco pesos, salí andando para Carlsbad. 4. Él se puso el sombrero antes de salir. 5. ¿Quiere Vd. cobrar el dinero antes de regresar a México? 6. Juan dijo que necesitaba más dinero. 7. María dijo que le faltaban cinco pesos para pagar el pasaje a St. Louis. 8. No me gusta trabajar cuando hace tanto frío. 9. ¿Le gustan a Vd. estos sacos nuevos que compré ayer? 10. Me gustan pero creo que Vd. pagó demasiado dinero por ellos. 11. El padre de él le hizo estudiar antes de ir al cine. 12. Él tuvo que hacer planchar una camisa antes de ir al baile.

EXERCISE

1. You ought to put on your coat before going to the office. 2. We have to return early because his aunt is ill. 3. He had a brick house made because it was very hot in the summer. 4. I do not like to ride horseback. 5. He does not like these shirts because they are silk. 6. We did not go on the bus because we needed more money. 7. Before buying a new car, why don't you sell the old one? 8. I do not want to sell my old car because it has four new tires and my son needs it in his business. 9. Many people do not like to work because they are lazy. 10. You ought to tell the truth all the time. 11. Riding horseback is good for your health (para la salud). 12. If you do not have the money, why don't you tell him that you will pay him tomorrow? 13. After meeting the man on the square, what did you do then?

ADVERBS

An adverb is a word that modifies a verb, an adjective, or another adverb. It is often formed by adding **"mente"** to the feminine singular form of the adjective.

Adjective		Adverb	
lenta	(slow)	lentamente	(slowly)
rápida	(rapid)	rápidamente	(rapidly)
feliz	(happy)	felizmente	(happily)
triste	(sad)	tristemente	(sadly)

Many times an adverbial phrase is used instead of the adverb.

Adverb	Adverbial phrase	Translation
finalmente	al fin, por fin	finally, at last
ciertamente	por cierto	certainly
claramente	con claridad	clearly
fácilmente	con facilidad	easily

Adverbs are compared as follows:

Positive	Comparative	Superlative
lentamente (slowly)	más lentamente (more slowly)	más lentamente (most slowly)
lentamente (slowly)	menos lentamente (less slowly)	menos lentamente (least slowly)

Some adverbs are compared irregularly:

bien	(well)	mejor	(better)	mejor	(best)
mal	(badly)	peor	(worse)	peor	(worst)
mucho	(much)	más	(more)	más	(most)
poco	(little)	menos	(less)	menos	(least)

Notice that in the superlative degree in the comparison of adverbs the definite article is not used as it is in the comparison of adjectives.

Ella canta muy bien.	She sings very well.
Él habla distintamente.	He speaks distinctly.

118

más—more
menos—less
ya—already
sin—without
así—thus, so
pues—well, then
entonces—then
por todas partes—everywhere
de cuando en cuando—from
   time to time

solo—alone
hasta luego—so long
hasta la vista—see you later
casi—nearly
siempre—always
luego—then, next
hoy día—nowadays
al fin, por fin—at last, finally
de vez en cuando—from time
   to time

EXERCISE

1. Ya he mandado el dinero a mis padres. 2. Él estudia más que Juan pero aprende menos porque siempre está pensando en otras cosas. 3. Ella se fué sin pagar la cuenta pero creo que la pagará dentro de unos pocos días. 4. Siempre hay mucho trabajo en los meses de mayo y junio porque es durante la cosecha. 5. Los rancheros (hacendados) plantan algodón en la primavera, lo desahijan en el verano, y lo piscan en el otoño. 6. Los piscadores ganan mucho dinero pero tienen que trabajar mucho. 7. Los caballos no se usan mucho en las haciendas hoy día; hay todas clases de máquinas para hacer el trabajo. 8. Los tractores son muy buenos pero cuestan mucho dinero y usan mucha gasolina y aceite. 9. No me gusta ir al cine los sábados; de vez en cuando voy los sábados por la tarde con mis hijos. 10. ¿Hasta cuando piensa Vd. quedarse en Del Río? 11. Quiero quedarme aquí como dos semanas, entonces voy al rancho de mi hijo quien casi siempre quede darme empleo. 12. ¿Quién le acompañó a Vd. a los Estados Unidos? 13. Nadie me acompañó; vine solo.

EXERCISE

1. Speak more slowly; I cannot understand you when you talk so fast. 2. I have already sold my car, and I will have to walk. 3. In what month did you leave Globe? 4. I do not remember, but they were picking cotton in the valley. 5. I worked for a man who has a garage in Ysleta. 6. I had been here two months before I got work. 7. I do not remember his name, but he was an American and lived on a farm near El Paso.

RELATIONSHIP OF WORDS

The following suggestions should be of help to a beginner in the study of the Spanish language. They are not complete by any means and should be remembered as general suggestions only.

Words which end in "tion" in English, end in "ción" in Spanish.

action—**acción**	nation—**nación**
attention—**atención**	addition—**adición**

The only double consonants found in Spanish are RR, LL, CC, and occasionally NN. The CH, LL, and RR are considered single letters and are never separated.

The prefix "im" in English becomes "in" in Spanish.

immortal—**inmortal**	immense—**inmenso**
immigration—**inmigración**	immoral—**inmoral**

Words starting with an "s" in English, followed by a consonant are started with "es" in Spanish.

Spanish—**español**	school—**escuela**
scale—**escala**	student—**estudiante**

The principal method of combining nouns is by placing the secondary noun last and connecting the two by **"de."**

traje de baile—balldress
jugo de limón—lemon juice
anillo de oro—gold ring
caballo de silla—saddle horse
molino de viento—windmill
traje de lana—woolen suit

If the secondary noun expresses purpose or use for which the first is intended, use **"para"** instead of **"de."**

estante para libros—bookcase
vaso para cerveza—beer glass
percha para sombreros—hat rack

An infinitive is often used as a verbal noun expressed in English by the gerund (see pages 115 and 116).

máquina de coser—sewing machine
pluma de dibujar—drawing pen
máquina de escribir—typewriter

"Ero" added to words of commerce forms the noun denoting the dealer in those articles, while "ería" added to those words denotes the shop or place of business.

zapato	**zapatero**	**zapatería**	**reloj**	**relojero**	**relojería**
shoe	shoemaker	shoe shop	watch	watchmaker	watch shop
leche	**lechero**	**lechería**	**joya**	**joyero**	**joyería**
milk	milkman	dairy	jewel	jeweler	jewelry shop

The names of many fruit trees ending in "o" change the "o" to "a" for the fruit.

cerezo	**cereza**	**naranjo**	**naranja**
cherry tree	cherry	orange tree	orange

The feminine form of a past participle often expresses the completed action of the verb from which it came.

llegar (to arrive)	**llegada** (arrival)
entrar (to enter)	**entrada** (entrance)
venir (to come)	**venida** (coming)
salir (to leave)	**salida** (leaving)

The following words, opposite in meaning, should be noted:

caballero (gentleman)	**dama** (lady)
caballo (horse)	**yegua** (mare)
yerno (son-in-law)	**nuera** (daughter-in-law)
toro (bull)	**vaca** (cow)

"Ito," "a"; "cito," "a"; "ecito," "a," when added to a noun convey the additional idea of sweet, nice, or little.

madrecita	dear mother	**hermanito**	little brother
pobrecito	poor little thing	**cabrito**	kid (little goat)
chiquito	very small	**perrito**	pup (little dog)

Proper names often add "ito," "ita," as follows:

Juan	**Juanito**	Johnny
Carlos	**Carlitos**	Charlie
Ana	**Anita**	Annie
Ricardo	**Ricardito**	Dickie

"Illo," "cillo," and "ecillo" are added to words to form diminutives:

campana	bell	**campanilla**	hand bell
muestra	sample	**muestrecilla**	little sample
chico	little	**chiquillo**	very little

121

Note the diminutive form of the following adjectives and adverbs:

ahora	now	**ahorita**	right now
pronto	soon	**prontito**	very soon
cerca	near	**cerquita**	quite near
poco	little	**poquito**	very little

Some nouns form the augmentatives by adding "ón" for the masculine and "ona" for the feminine.

hombre	man	**hombrón**	large man
mujer	woman	**mujerona**	large woman
soltera	woman (single)	**solterona**	woman (old maid)
zapatos	shoes	**zapatones**	very large shoes

English verbs ending in "ate" generally end in "ar" in Spanish.

calculate	**calcular**	conjugate	**conjugar**
terminate	**terminar**	celebrate	**celebrar**
imitate	**imitar**	indicate	**indicar**

Verbs ending in "fy" in English generally end in "ficar" in Spanish.

certify	**certificar**	clarify	**clarificar**
fortify	**fortificar**	identify	**identificar**

English adjectives ending in "ate" generally end in "ado" in Spanish.

duplicate—**duplicado**
moderate—**moderado**
subordinate—**subordinado**

Verbs ending in "ize" in English usually end in "izar" in Spanish.

authorize	**autorizar**	analyze	**analizar**
colonize	**colonizar**	dramatize	**dramatizar**

"Contestar" and **"responder"** require "a" before a following object.

Contesto a la carta.	I answer the letter.
Responde a las preguntas.	He responds to the questions.

"Comprar" and **"pedir"** require "a" instead of "de" before a following noun or pronoun.

Compro mis vestidos al señor García.	I buy my clothes from Mr. Garcia.
Pido dinero a mi padre.	I ask my father for money.

Indirect object nouns require "a" (sometimes omitted in English).

Yo escribí una carta a Pablo.	I wrote Paul a letter.
Él mandó un libro a María.	He sent Mary a book.

Certain Spanish verbs include the English preposition.

escuchar—to listen to		**mirar**—to look at
esperar—to wait for		**sacar**—to take out
buscar—to look for		**pedir**—to ask for

Verbs of motion, teaching, learning, and beginning require **"a"** before a following infinitive.

ir—to go	**Voy a estudiar.**	I am going to study.
aprender—to learn	**Él aprende a leer.**	He is learning to read.
enseñar—to teach	**Yo le enseño a leer.**	I teach you to read.
empezar—to begin	**Él empezó a hablar.**	He began to speak.

Some verbs require **"de"** before a following infinitive, noun, or pronoun.

acordarse de—to remember	acabar de—to have just
tratar de—to try to	cesar de—to cease to

No me acuerdo de él.	I don't remember him.
Acabo de estudiar mi lección.	I have just studied my lesson.
Él trató de hacerlo.	He tried to do it.
Él cesó de hacerlo.	He stopped doing it.

A few verbs require **"en"** before a following infinitive.

insistir en—to insist	tardar en—to be late
convenir en—to agree on	fijarse en—to pay attention to

Él insiste en hacerlo.	He insists on doing it.
Él no tardó en llegar.	He was not late in arriving.
Él convino en pagarme.	He agreed to pay me.
Fíjese Vd. en esto.	(You) pay attention to this.

APPENDIX

IDIOMATIC EXPRESSIONS

tener años—to be years of age
tener calor—to be warm
tener la culpa—to be to blame
tener cuidado—to be careful
tener dolor de—to have an ache
tener éxito—to be successful
tener frío—to be cold
tener ganas de—to be desirous of (feel like)
tener gusto en—to be glad to
tener hambre—to be hungry
tener miedo—to be afraid
tener lugar—to take place
tener sed—to be thirsty
tener sueño—to be sleepy
tener prisa—to be in a hurry
tener razón—to be right
no tener razón—to be wrong
tener vergüenza—to be ashamed
tener que (plus infinitive)—to have to
tener a la vista—to keep in sight
tener puesto—to have on
tener presente—to bear in mind
tener en cuenta—to bear in mind
tener que ver con—to have to do with
tener por—to consider as

hacer buen tiempo—to be good weather
hacer años—years ago
hacer (plus period of time)—ago
hacer calor—to be warm
hacer frío—to be cold
hacer fresco—to be cool
hacer sol—to be shining (sun)
hacer luna—to be shining (moon)
hacer mal tiempo—to be bad weather
hacer una pregunta—to ask a question
hacer una visita—to make a visit
hacer un viaje—to make (take) a trip
hacer viento (aire)—to be windy

hacer arreglos—to make arrangements
hacer pedazos—to break to pieces
hacer juramento—to swear
hacerle la primera cura a—to render first-aid to
hacerse—to become
hacer caso de—to heed, pay attention to
hacerse cargo de—to take charge of

ponerse—to put on
ponerse—to become
llegar a ser—to become
ponerse a—to begin to
ponerse enfermo—to become ill
ponerse en pie—to stand
poner una queja—to file a complaint
poner una queja—to file charges (suit)
poner la mesa—set the table
levantar la mesa—to clear the table
volverse loco—to go crazy
volver a (plus infinitive)—to do again
volver corriendo—to run back

hay—there is, are
hay luna—the moon shines
hay sol—the sun shines
hay lodo—it is muddy
hay polvo—it is dusty
está airoso—it is windy
hay que (plus infinitive)—it is necessary to, one must
hay quienes—there are those who

dar a—to face
dar con—to meet (happen upon)
dar de comer—to feed
dar la hora—to strike the hour
dar las gracias—to thank
dar un paseo—to take a walk
dar una vuelta—to take a stroll (walk)

darse prisa—to hurry
dar atención—to pay attention
dar en—to hit
dar fianza por—to give bail for
dar la mano a—to shake hands
dar la vuelta a—to turn
el año pasado—last year
el año que viene—next year
el año próximo—next year
el año entrante—next year
el año que entra—next year
por primera vez—for the first time
de día—in the daytime, by day
de noche—at night, by night
ocho días—a week
una semana—a week
quince días—two weeks
dos semanas—two weeks
ayer por la tarde—yesterday afternoon
ayer por la mañana—yesterday morning
mañana por la mañana—tomorrow morning
mañana por la tarde—tomorrow afternoon
mañana por la noche—tomorrow night

mediodía—noon
medianoche—midnight
Es mediodía.—It is noon.
Es medianoche.—It is midnight.
al anochecer—at dusk
al amanecer—at dawn
a la caída de la tarde—at nightfall
a la caída del sol—at sunset
a la madrugada—early morning
¿Qué hora es?—What time is it?
¿Qué horas son?—What time is it? (colloquial)
¿a qué hora?—at what time?
al fin del año—at the end of the year
al principio del año—at the beginning of the year
al último del mes—at the end of the month
a últimos del mes—toward the end of the month
a ratos—at times (occasionally)
de vez en cuando—from time to time

Es tarde.—It is late.
Es temprano.—It is early.

un buen rato—a good while
a eso de las dos—at about two o'clock
más o menos a las dos—at about two o'clock
como a las dos—at about two o'clock
a cosa de las dos—at about two o'clock
hace poco—a little while ago

a menudo—often
a tiempo—on time (but) con tiempo—ahead of time
de pronto—suddenly
a pie—on foot

de pie—standing
a todo correr—at full speed
a toda velocidad—at full speed
calle arriba—up the street
calle abajo—down the street

de aquí en adelante—from now on
de hoy en adelante—from now on
de ahí en adelante—from that time on
de aquel tiempo en adelante—from that time on
desde entonces en adelante—from then on
es la hora de—it is time to

¿Qué día del mes tenemos?—What day of the month is it?
¿A cuántos estamos?—What day of the month is it?
¿A cómo estamos?—What day of the month is it?
¿Cuál es la fecha de hoy?—What is the date today?

en seguida—immediately
ahora mismo—right now
¿Qué ha sido de . . . ?—What has become of . . . ?
¿Qué se ha hecho de . . . ?—What has become of . . . ?

perder de vista—to lose sight of
perder el tren—to miss the train
acabar de (plus infinitive)—to have just
estar para (plus infinitive)—to be about to
montar a caballo—to ride horseback

dejar de (plus infinitive)—to fail to
dejar caer—to drop
estar de vuelta—to be back
querer decir—to mean
apresúrese Vd.—hurry
ándale—hurry
córrele—hurry
dése Vd. prisa—hurry
dispénseme Vd.—pardon (excuse) me
perdóneme Vd.—pardon (excuse) me
con permiso—pardon (excuse) me
estar por (plus infinitive)—to be in favor of

Creo que sí.—I think so.
Creo que no.—I think not.
Ya lo creo.—Yes, indeed.
¿de veras?—really?
segura que sí—it is positively so or right
de buena gana—gladly
de memoria—by heart (memory)
de moda—stylish, fashionable
en cuanto a—concerning, as for, as to
tocante a—concerning, as for, as to
respecto a—concerning, as for, as to
en vez de—instead of
a veces—at times
a la vez—at the same time
tal vez—perhaps
No hay de qué.—You are welcome.
por nada—you are welcome
de nada—you are welcome
otra vez—again
de nuevo—again
lomas de arena—sand hills
¿De qué tamaño es?—What size is it?
¿Para qué se usa?—What is it used for?
¿Para qué sirve?—What is it used for?
¿Para qué lo usan?—What is it used for?
a gatas—on all fours
a cuestas—on one's shoulders (back)
tardar en—to be long in
prendas de vestir—articles of clothing
es nacido—is born
fué nacido—was born
poco más o menos—about (more or less)
Mande Vd.—I did not understand you.
¿Cómo no?—Why not? To be sure.
a casa—home (motion)
en casa—at home

hace dos días—two days ago
al derecho—straight ahead
a la derecha—to the right
a la izquierda—to the left
lo más pronto posible—as soon as possible
de vuelta—again
hasta la vista—goodbye, until we meet again
hasta luego—goodbye, until we meet again
Nos estamos viendo.—I'll be seeing you.
Que le vaya bien.—Good luck.
Que vaya con Dios.—God be with you.
Que lo pase bien.—Good luck (for the day or night).
tenga la bondad de—please
haga el favor de—please
Sírvase Vd.—Please.
por favor—please
poco a poco—little by little
de este modo—in this manner

vamos a ver—let's see
más que nunca—more than ever
Es (la) hora de comer.—It is dinnertime.
fijarse en—to notice
todo el mundo—everybody
por todas partes—everywhere
un poco de—a little
dentro de poco—in a short time
por lo menos—at least
prestar atención—to pay attention
salir bien (mal) en—to be successful (unsuccessful)
sentar bien a—to fit well (clothes)
caer bien a—to fit well
Le está bien.—It fits him well.
ni yo tampoco—nor I either
en voz alta—aloud
en voz baja—in a low voice
al contado—cash, for cash
al fiado—on credit
en abonos—on installment, on credit
valer la pena—to be worth while
No vale la pena.—It is not worth while.
echar al correo—to mail
ir de compras—to go shopping
vale más que—it would be better if
de punto—just right
ir al centro—to go down town

expendio de gasolina—gasoline (filling) station
estación de gasolina—gasoline (filling) station
depósito de gasolina—gasoline tank
tren de carga—freight train
carro (vagón) de carga—freight car
furgón—freight car
carguero—freight car
¿Qué pasó?—What happened?
a lo largo de—along
al fin—at last
por fin—at last
Está bien (bueno).—It's all right.
por aquí—this way
Pase Vd. por aquí.—Come this way.
ser culpable de—to be guilty of
Se hace tarde.—It is getting late.
Se hace noche.—It is getting dark.
Eso es.—That's right.
a lado de—beside, next to
al otro lado—on the other side
a obscuras—at night, in the dark
alto—halt, stop

trastos de cocina—kitchen utensils
atrasado—behind, delayed
por eso—for that reason
hoy día—nowadays
de tren—by train
algo que comer—something to eat
pan duro—stale bread
pan frío—stale bread
por supuesto—of course
sala de espera—waiting room
estar bien de salud—to be in good health
tan de prisa—so fast
tan aprisa—so fast
con su permiso—excuse me
cambiarse de ropa—to change clothes
mudar de ropa—to change clothes
mudar de casa—to move (to change residence)
cambiar de casa—to move (to change residence)
recibir noticias de—to hear from
decir para sí—to say to oneself
es decir—that is to say
se dice—it is said

PRACTICE MATERIAL

Tengo las manos frías.	My hands are cold.
Él tiene los pies fríos.	His feet are cold.
Ella tiene los ojos azules.	Her eyes are blue.
¿Qué tiene Vd.?	What is the matter with you?
¿Cuántos años tiene Vd.?	How old are you?
¿Qué edad tiene Vd.?	How old are you?
Habrá mucha gente aquí.	There will be a lot of people here.
¿Está su papá? Sí, señor, pase Vd.	Is your papa at home? Yes, sir, come in.
Mi reloj anda atrasado.	My watch is slow.
¿Qué tanto tiempo tiene Vd. aquí?	How long have you lived here?
No caben muchos alumnos en este cuarto.	This room will not hold many students.
Me duelen los ojos.	My eyes hurt.
Él se puso a reparar el reloj.	He set to work repairing the watch.
Él no tardó en llegar.	He was not long in arriving.
Tengo gusto en conocerle.	I am glad to know you.
Le presento al señor Jones.	This is Mr. Jones.
Éste es el señor Jones.	This is Mr. Jones.
Después supe que él era ciudadano de México.	Then I found out that he was a citizen of Mexico.
Allá voy, señor.	I'm coming, sir.
Ya voy.	I'm going right now.

¿Qué tan lejos está?	How far is it?
¿Qué distancia hay de Juárez a El Paso?	How far is it from Juarez to El Paso?
¿Cuántas millas hay de Juárez a El Paso?	How many miles is it from Juarez to El Paso?
No tuve oportunidad de hacerlo.	I didn't have a chance to do it.
¿Qué tanto (cuánto) tiempo se quedó (pasó) Vd. allí?	How long did you stay over there?
Él se puso a correr.	He began to run.
El carro se puso en marcha.	The car started.
Ella está bien de salud.	She is in good health.
Él pegó fuego a la casa.	He set the house on fire.
Ella se puso enojada.	She became angry.
Él se hizo rico.	He became rich.
Me puse el sombrero.	I put on my hat.
Póngase Vd. en pie.	Stand up.
Estamos muy atrasados porque mi esposo no tiene trabajo.	We are very much behind (set back) because my husband does not have work.
Pase Vd. por aquí.	Come this way.
Se prohibe estacionarse aquí.	Parking is prohibited here.
No hable tan aprisa.	Do not talk so fast.
¿En qué se ocupa Vd.?	What is your occupation?
¿Cuál es su nacionalidad?	What is your nationality?
¿De qué nacionalidad es Vd.?	What is your nationality?
Me impusieron una multa de $5.00.	They fined me $5.00.
Le tengo por hombre.	I consider him a man.
Le vimos cruzar el río.	We saw him cross the river.
Subí a lo alto de la loma de arena.	I climbed to the top of the sand hill.
Yo entré en el automóvil hace poco.	I entered the automobile not long ago.
Tomamos un poco de agua.	We drank a little water.
Lo vendí en veinte pesos.	I sold it for twenty pesos.
El hombre acaba de entrar.	The man has just entered.
Eso está bien.	That is all right.
Creo que sí, pero él cree que no.	I think so, but he does not believe so.
¿Llovió mucho ayer?	Did it rain much yesterday?
¡Ya lo creo!	I should say so!
Ella cumplió diez (años) ayer.	She was ten years old yesterday.
Dieron las tres hace rato.	It struck three (o'clock) a short time ago.
Mi casa da al norte.	My house faces the north.
Dimos un paseo en automóvil.	We took an automobile ride.
Lo hice de buena gana.	I did it gladly.
Su traje es muy de moda.	His suit is very stylish.
Él me dejó entrar.	He let me enter.
Ellos dejaron de venir.	They failed to come.
Voy a escribirla desde luego.	I am going to write it at once.
Él trabajó todo el día.	He worked all day.
Iremos los dos a visitarle.	We shall both go to visit her.
Vd. se equivoca.	You are mistaken.
Él salió mucho tiempo ha.	He left a long while ago.
Apresúrese Vd., se hace tarde.	Hurry, it is getting late.

Me parece que es culpa suya.	I think (it seems to me) that it is your fault.
Por malo que sea, es honesto.	However bad he is, he is honest.
Me quedan dos dólares.	I have two dollars left.
Seguimos escribiendo.	We continued writing.
Es la hora de comer.	It is time to eat.
¿No se siente Vd. bien?	Don't you feel well?
Yo me serví de su carro.	I used your car.
Tengo dolor de cabeza.	I have a headache.
Ahora me toca a mí decir algo.	Now it is my turn to say something.
Quiero decirle algo a Vd.	I want to tell you something.
La boda tuvo lugar ayer.	The marriage took place yesterday.
Ella lo dijo en voz baja.	She said it in a whisper.
Ya no fuma él.	He no longer smokes.
No tenemos nada que vender.	We have nothing to sell.
Él salió de aquí muy de mañana.	He left here early in the morning.

EXERCISE

En la Sala de Espera

Acabamos de llegar a la estación. El tren de Chicago ha de llegar a la seis y ahora faltan diez para las seis. El tren no llegó hasta las seis y media. Mucha gente baja del tren. Algunos van a quedarse en El Paso, y otros quieren tomar algo que comer o beber antes de la salida del tren a las siete y cuarto. Todo el mundo está muy ocupado. Los porteros meten las maletas en los automóviles. Un hombre viejo va al teléfono y llama un taxi. El viejo sube al carro y dice—Al Hotel Colón. —El chofer guía (maneja) el carro con cuidado porque no quiere chocar con otro carro. Hay muchos choques en las ciudades grandes.

Nos fijamos en (Notamos) un hombre que está sentado en la sala de espera leyendo un diario. Él está bien vestido. Lleva sombrero azul, traje gris, camisa de color, corbata listada, y zapatos negros. Le saludamos y empezamos a platicar. Nos dice que es dueño de una mina en Toltec, México, y ha venido a los Estados Unidos para comprar unos motores, y otra maquinaria. Su permiso es válido por tres semanas. Él va a Denver para hacer las compras y entonces piensa regresar a México por el puerto de Nogales. Nos despedimos de él y hablamos con otros.

Idioms

acabar de (plus) infinitive—to have just
haber de (plus) infinitive—to be to, must
algo que comer o beber—something to eat or drink
estar ocupado—to be busy
con cuidado—carefully
fijarse en—to notice
hacer compras—to shop, to make purchases
sala de espera—waiting room

SPANISH NAMES

Spanish and Spanish-American people usually use the surname of both parents. Neither is ever considered to be a middle name.

The surname of the father precedes that of the mother and the two surnames may or may not be joined by the conjunction "y" (and) or by a hyphen. Example: **Juan Romero y Conde, Juan Romero-Conde, Juan Romero Conde. Juan** is the given name, **Romero** the surname of the father and **Conde** the surname of the mother.

In addition, the following variations may be found:

Juan Conde Romero	**Juan Romero C.**
Juan C. Romero	**Juan Romero**
Juan Conde	

Legally, a Spanish female retains her maiden name after marriage, but it is common practice to drop the surname of the mother and to add that of the husband joined by the preposition **"de"** (of).

For example: **Luisa Romero y Conde** marries **Carlos Villa y Tovar** and is known as **Luisa Romero de Villa.**

Prior to her marriage she was known as:	**Luisa Romero y Conde,**
after marriage as:	**Luisa Romero de Villa,**
and, should her husband die, as:	**Luisa Romero Vda. de Villa.**
	(**Vda., viuda**—widow)

Spanish words are more phonetic than English words. However, due to similarity of the sounds of certain letters, differences in the spelling of proper names will be encountered. Examples of a few of these instances follow:

Letters	Names
s–c	**Seballos**—Ceballos
b–v	**Baca**—Vaca
c–z	**Celaya**—Zelaya
s–z	**Sambrano**—Zambrano
ll–y	**Calletano**—Cayetano
j–h	**Jaro**—Haro
i–e	**Arriola**—Arreola
g–j	**Guantez**—Juantes
rr–r	**Arredondo**—Aredondo
h	Any name with "h"
i–y	**Ibarra**—Ybarra

The prepositions **"de,"** with or without a definite article, "el," etc., appear in a number of Spanish surnames. Formerly the preposition **"de"** was an indication of nobility, but today such a distinction does not exist, and the use of **"de"** is optional. However, it is retained by some families as a part of the surname. Examples: **De Haro, De Lora, Del Campo, Del Valle, De la Torre, De la Rosa, De la O.**

REGULAR VERBS

The Three Conjugations

FIRST CONJUGATION AR

Present participle	Infinitive	Past participle
habl ando	**habl ar**	**habl ado**

INDICATIVE MOOD

Present

yo habl o	I speak, am speaking, do speak
tú habl as	you speak, are speaking, do speak
él, ella, Vd. habl a	he, she, you speak, do speak, etc.
nosotros, as habl amos	we speak, are speaking, do speak
vosotros, as habl áis	you speak, are speaking, do speak
ellos, as, Vds. habl an	they (m–f), you speak, etc.

Imperfect

yo habl aba	I used to speak, was speaking
tú habl abas	you used to speak, were speaking
él, ella, Vd. habl aba	he, she, you used to speak, etc.
nosotros, as habl ábamos	we used to speak, were speaking
vosotros, as habl abais	you used to speak, were speaking
ellos, as, Vds. habl aban	they (m–f), you used to speak, etc.

Preterite

yo habl é	I spoke, did speak
tú habl aste	you spoke, did speak
él, ella, Vd. habl ó	he, she, you spoke, etc.
nosotros, as habl amos	we spoke, did speak
vosotros, as habl asteis	you spoke, did speak
ellos, as, Vds. habl aron	they (m–f), you spoke, etc.

Future

yo hablar é	I shall or will speak
tú hablar ás	you shall or will speak
él, ella, Vd. hablar á	he, she, you will or shall speak, etc.
nosotros, as hablar emos	we shall or will speak
vosotros, as hablar éis	you shall or will speak
ellos, as, Vds. hablar án	they (m–f), you shall speak, etc.

Conditional

yo hablar ía	I should or would speak
tú hablar ías	you should or would speak
él, ella, Vd. hablar ía	he, she, you would or should speak, etc.

nosotros, as hablar íamos	we should or would speak
vosotros, as hablar íais	you should or would speak
ellos, as, Vds. hablar ían	they (m–f), you would or should speak, etc.

SECOND CONJUGATION ER   THIRD CONJUGATION IR

Present participle

| com iendo | recib iendo |

Infinitive

| com er | recib ir |

Past participle

| com ido | recib ido |

INDICATIVE MOOD

Present

com o	recib o
com es	recib es
com e	recib e
com emos	recib imos
com éis	recib ís
com en	recib en

Imperfect

com ía	recib ía
com ías	recib ías
com ía	recib ía
com íamos	recib íamos
com íais	recib íais
com ían	recib ían

Preterite

com í	recib í
com iste	recib iste
com ió	recib ió
com imos	recib imos
com isteis	recib isteis
com ieron	recib ieron

Future

comer é	recibir é
comer ás	recibir ás
comer á	recibir á
comer emos	recibir emos
comer éis	recibir éis
comer án	recibir án

comer ía	recibir ía
comer ías	recibir ías
comer ía	recibir ía
comer íamos	recibir íamos
comer íais	recibir íais
comer ían	recibir ían

THE COMPOUND TENSES

THE COMPOUND TENSES OF THE INDICATIVE MOOD

The compound tenses are formed by conjugating the auxiliary verb "haber" in the proper tense preceding the best participle of the main verb.

First Conjugation AR

Infinitive

haber habl ado—to have spoken

Participle

habiendo habl ado—having spoken

INDICATIVE MOOD

Present perfect

yo he habl ado	I have spoken
tú has habl ado	you have spoken
él, ella, Vd. ha habl ado	he has, she has, you have spoken
nosotros, as hemos habl ado	we have spoken
vosotros, as habéis habl ado	you have spoken
ellos, as, Vds. han habl ado	they (m–f), you have spoken

Pluperfect (past perfect)[24]

[24] The preterite perfect has been omitted throughout this work and is, therefore, omitted in this treatment of verbs. The simple preterite may replace the preterite perfect at any time. Any time a past perfect is needed the pluperfect may be used.

yo había habl ado	I had spoken
tú habías habl ado	you had spoken
él, ella, Vd. había habl ado	he, she, you had spoken
nosotros, as habíamos habl ado	we had spoken
vosotros, as habíais habl ado	you had spoken
ellos, as, Vds. habían habl ado	they (m–f), you had spoken

Future perfect

yo habré habl ado	I shall or will have spoken
tú habrás habl ado	you shall or will have spoken
él, ella, Vd. habrá habl ado	he, she, you will or shall, etc.

133

nosotros, as habremos habl ado	we shall or will have spoken
vosotros, as habréis habl ado	you shall or will have spoken
ellos, as, Vds. habrán habl ado	they (m–f), you will or shall, etc.

Conditional perfect

yo habría habl ado	I should or would have spoken
tú habrías habl ado	you should or would have spoken
él, ella, Vd. habría habl ado	he, she, you would or should have, etc.

nosotros, as habríamos habl ado	we should or would have spoken
vosotros, as habríais habl ado	you should or would have spoken
ellos, as, Vds. habrían habl ado	they (m–f), you would or should have, etc.

Second Conjugation ER   Third Conjugation IR

Infinitive

haber com ido   haber recib ido

Participle

habiendo com ido   habiendo recib ido

INDICATIVE MOOD

Present perfect

he com ido	he recib ido
has com ido	has recib ido
ha com ido	ha recib ido
hemos com ido	hemos recib ido
habéis com ido	habéis recib ido
han com ido	han recib ido

Pluperfect (past perfect)

había com ido	había recib ido
habías com ido	habías recib ido
había com ido	había recib ido
habíamos com ido	habíamos recib ido
habíais com ido	habíais recib ido
habían com ido	habían recib ido

Future perfect

habré com ido	habré recib ido
habrás com ido	habrás recib ido
habrá com ido	habrá recib ido
habremos com ido	habremos recib ido
habréis com ido	habréis recib ido
habrán com ido	habrán recib ido

Conditional perfect

habría com ido	habría recib ido
habrías com ido	habrías recib ido
habría com ido	habría recib ido

habríamos com ido	habríamos recib ido
habríais com ido	habríais recib ido
habrían com ido	habrían recib ido

SUBJUNCTIVE MOOD

First Conjugation	Second Conjugation	Third Conjugation

Present

Hablar	*Comer*	*Recibir*
habl e	com a	recib a
habl es	com as	recib as
habl e	com a	recib a
habl emos	com amos	recib amos
habl éis	com áis	recib áis
habl en	com an	recib an

Imperfect "ra" form

habl ara	com iera	recib iera
habl aras	com ieras	recib ieras
habl ara	com iera	recib iera
habl áramos	com iéramos	recib iéramos
habl arais	com ierais	recib ierais
habl aran	com ieran	recib ieran

Imperfect "se" form

habl ase	com iese	recib iese
habl ases	com ieses	recib ieses
habl ase	com iese	recib iese
habl ásemos	com iésemos	recib iésemos
habl aseis	com ieseis	recib ieseis
habl asen	com iesen	recib iesen

THE COMPOUND TENSES OF THE SUBJUNCTIVE MOOD

Present perfect

haya hablado	haya comido	haya recibido
hayas hablado	hayas comido	hayas recibido
haya hablado	haya comido	haya recibido
hayamos hablado	hayamos comido	hayamos recibido
hayáis hablado	hayáis comido	hayáis recibido
hayan hablado	hayan comido	hayan recibido

Pluperfect "ra"

hubiera hablado	hubiera comido	hubiera recibido
hubieras hablado	hubieras comido	hubieras recibido
hubiera hablado	hubiera comido	hubiera recibido

135

Pluperfect "ra"

hubiéramos hablado	hubiéramos comido	hubiéramos recibido
hubierais hablado	hubierais comido	hubierais recibido
hubieran hablado	hubieran comido	hubieran recibido

Pluperfect "se"

hubiese hablado	hubiese comido	hubiese recibido
hubieses hablado	hubieses comido	hubieses recibido
hubiese hablado	hubiese comido	hubiese recibido
hubiésemos hablado	hubiésemos comido	hubiésemos recibido
hubieseis hablado	hubieseis comido	hubieseis recibido
hubiesen hablado	hubiesen comido	hubiesen recibido

IMPERATIVE MOOD[25]

habla tú	come tú	recibe tú
hablad vosotros	comed vosotros	recibid vosotros

SUBJUNCTIVE-IMPERATIVE[25]

hable Vd.	coma Vd.	reciba Vd.
hablen Vds.	coman Vds.	reciban Vds.

ORTHOGRAPHICALLY CHANGING VERBS

In Spanish the sound of the final consonant of the stem of the infinitive is generally maintained throughout the conjugation of the verb. In order to do so, it is sometimes necessary to make certain changes in the spelling (orthography) of the stem before attaching the endings. Pronouncing the word will often help the beginner to identify the verb as orthographically changing rather than irregular. The following paragraphs list these changes. The orthographical changes are shown in capital letters in the examples following the rules.

RULES FOR MAKING ORTHOGRAPHICAL CHANGES IN VERBS

1. c of car changes to qu before e.
2. g of gar changes to gu before e.
3. gu of guar changes to gü before e.

[25] The imperative mood is used for the familiar command. The third person singular and plural of the subjunctive is used for the polite command. Some grammarians call this use of the subjunctive the "subjunctive-imperative" as so designated above. The negative familiar command uses the second person of the present subjunctive instead of the imperative.

4. g of ger and gir changes to j before a or o.
5. gu of guir drops the u before a or o.
6. qu of quir changes to c before a or o.
7. z of zar changes to c before e.
8. cer and cir preceded by a consonant change c to z before a or o.
9. ll and ñ followed by ie or ió drop the i.
10. i unaccented between two vowels changes to y.
11. cer and cir preceded by a vowel insert z before c before a or o.
12. uir unless u is silent, insert y before a, e, or o (strengthens).
13. iar and uar require the written accent mark (′) over the i or u in the 1st, 2nd, and 3rd person singular, and 3rd person plural of the present indicative and present subjunctive and the singular imperative. This is not true of all verbs ending in iar and uar.

EXAMPLES

1. Buscar

Preterite indicative	Present subjunctive
busQUé	busQUe
buscaste	busQUes
buscó	busQUe
buscamos	busQUemos
buscasteis	busQUéis
buscaron	busQUen

2. Llegar

Preterite indicative	Present subjunctive
lleGUé	lleGUe
llegaste	lleGUes
llegó	lleGUe
llegamos	lleGUemos
llegasteis	lleGUéis
llegaron	lleGUen

3. Averiguar

Preterite indicative	Present subjunctive
averiGÜé	averiGÜe
averiguaste	averiGÜes
averiguó	averiGÜe
averiguamos	averiGÜemos
averiguasteis	averiGÜéis
averiguaron	averiGÜen

4. Coger

Present indicative	Present subjunctive
coJo	coJa
coges	coJas
coge	coJa
cogemos	coJamos
cogéis	coJáis
cogen	coJan

5. Distinguir

Present indicative	Present subjunctive
distinGo	distinGa
distingues	distinGas
distingue	distinGa
distinguimos	distinGamos
distinguís	distinGáis
distinguen	distinGan

6. Delinquir

Present indicative	Present subjunctive
delinCo	delinCa
delinques	delinCas
delinque	delinCa
delinquimos	delinCamos
delinquís	delinCáis
delinquen	delinCan

7. Empezar

Preterite indicative	Present subjunctive
empeCé	empieCe
empezaste	empieCes
empezó	empieCe
empezamos	empeCemos
empezasteis	empeCéis
empezaron	empieCen

8. Vencer

Present indicative	Present subjunctive
venZo	venZa
vences	venZas
vence	venZa
vencemos	venZamos
vencéis	venZáis
vencen	venZan

9. Bullir

Preterite indicative	Present participle
bullí	bull(i)endo
bulliste	
bull(i)ó	
bullimos	
bullisteis	
bull(i)eron	

10. Leer

Preterite indicative	Present participle
leí	leYendo
leíste	
leYó	
leímos	
leísteis	
leYeron	

11. Conocer

Present indicative	Present subjunctive
conoZco	conoZca
conoces	conoZcas
conoce	conoZca
conocemos	conoZcamos
conocéis	conoZcáis
conocen	conoZcan

12. Construir

Present indicative	Present subjunctive	Preterite indicative	Present participle	Imperative
construYo	construYa	construí	construYendo	construYe
construYes	construYas	construiste		
construYe	construYa	construYó		
construimos	construYamos	construimos		
construís	construYáis	construisteis		
construYen	construYan	construYeron		

13. Enviar

Present indicative	Present subjunctive	Imperative
envío	envíe	
envías	envíes	envía
envía	envíe	
enviamos	enviemos	
enviáis	enviéis	enviad
envían	envíen	

IRREGULAR VERBS

Present ind.	Present subj.	Imp. ind.	Pret. ind.	Fut. ind.	Cond. ind.	Imp.
			andar			
caber	caber		caber	caber	caber	
caer	caer					
			conducir			
dar	dar		dar			
decir	decir		decir	decir	decir	decir
estar	estar		estar			
haber	haber		haber	haber	haber	
hacer	hacer		hacer	hacer	hacer	hacer
ir	ir	ir	ir			ir
oír	oír					
			poder	poder	poder	
poner	poner		poner	poner	poner	poner
			querer	querer	querer	
saber	saber		saber	saber	saber	
salir	salir			salir	salir	salir
ser	ser	ser	ser			
tener	tener		tener	tener	tener	tener
traer	traer		traer			
valer	valer			valer	valer	valer
venir	venir		venir	venir	venir	venir
ver	ver	ver				

There are only twenty-two irregular verbs in common use in the Spanish language. Notice in the above table that many of these verbs are irregular in several tenses, but that none are irregular in all tenses.

In the present indicative tense eighteen of them are irregular. "Haber," "ir," and "ser" are completely irregular in this tense. "Estar" bears the written accent in the third person singular and plural. All others are irregular only in the first person singular, and with the exception of "dar" and "saber" the irregularity appears only in the stem of the verb. The endings are regular. "Decir," "tener," and "venir" follow the rule for radical changing verbs in the second and third persons singular and the third person plural.

The same eighteen verbs are also irregular in the present subjunctive tense. All others are regular in this tense. Only "haber," "ir," "saber," and "ser" are completely irregular. "Dar" and "estar" are regular except for the written accent. The remaining twelve verbs are conjugated in this tense by attaching the regular present subjunctive endings to the irregular stem of the first person singular of the present indicative.

In the imperfect indicative tense "ser," "ir," and "ver" are the only verbs that are irregular. "Ver" is irregular only in that it retains the "e" of the infinitive ending before attaching the regular endings.

There are seventeen verbs irregular in the preterite indicative tense. Fourteen of these have the same irregular endings that are attached to an irregular stem. "Ser" and "ir" are conjugated alike in this tense. "Dar" is irregular in that it is conjugated like a regular verb of the second or third conjugation.

There are twelve verbs that are irregular in the future indicative tense. The irregularity appears only in the stem of the verb.

The same twelve verbs are irregular in the conditional tense and to the same extent.

There are only eight verbs that are irregular in the imperative mood (familiar command). They are irregular in the singular. "Valer" has two familiar singular forms; "val," irregular and "vale," regular.

The imperfect subjunctive has not been listed as irregular as it may be conjugated by attaching the regular endings to the stem of the third person plural of the preterite indicative; however, the following two rules for orthographically changing verbs must be kept in mind:

(1) An unaccented "i" between two vowels is changed to "y."
Leer—leyera, leyeras, leyera, leyéramos, leyerais, leyeran
Caer—cayera, cayeras, cayera, cayéramos, cayerais, cayeran

(2) Those verbs whose stem ends in "j" drop the "i" of the imperfect subjunctive endings.
Traer—trajera, trajeras, trajera, trajéramos, trajerais, trajeran
Decir—dijera, dijeras, dijera, dijéramos, dijerais, dijeran

A simplified rule to follow in forming the imperfect subjunctive is: Drop the "ron" from the third person plural of the preterite indicative tense and to the remaining stem attach the following endings:

First or "ra" form: ra, ras, ra, ramos, rais, ran
Second or "se" form: se, ses, se semos, seis, sen

The verb "reír" (page 143) is an orthographically changing verb, but because it undergoes so many changes it has been conjugated, but not listed as irregular, with this group of verbs.

The compounds of these verbs are irregular to the same extent as the "parent" verb; that is, "obtener" has the same irregularities as "tener."

In the following conjugations of the irregular verbs regular tenses are not conjugated. However, if a verb is orthographically changing, it will be conjugated in such tense or tenses.

Verbs that have irregular past participles are not shown in the table on page 139, but are listed in the following conjugations. Verbs that appear to be irregular in the present participle are either orthographically changing verbs or radically changing verbs of the third classification.

140

ANDAR

Preterite indicative	**anduve, anduviste, anduvo, anduvimos, andu**[cut] **vieron**

CABER

Present indicative	**quepo, cabes, cabe, cabemos, cabéis, caben**
Present subjunctive	**quepa, quepas, quepa, quepamos, quepáis, quepan**
Preterite indicative	**cupe, cupiste, cupo, cupimos, cupisteis, cupieron**
Future indicative	**cabré, cabrás, cabrá, cabremos, cabréis, cabrán**
Conditional	**cabría, cabrías, cabría, cabríamos, cabríais, cabrían**

CAER

Present indicative	**caigo, caes, cae, caemos, caéis, caen**
Present subjunctive	**caiga, caigas, caiga, caigamos, calgáis, caigan**
Preterite indicative	**caí, caíste, cayó, caímos, caísteis, cayeron**
Present participle	**cayendo**
Past participle	**caído**

CONDUCIR

Present indicative	**conduzco, conduces, conduce, conducimos, conducís, conducen**
Present subjunctive	**conduzca, conduzcas, conduzca, conduzcamos, conduzcáis, conduzcan**
Preterite indicative	**conduje, condujiste, condujo, condujimos, condujisteis, condujeron**

DAR

Present indicative	**doy, das, da, damos, dais, dan**
Present subjunctive	**dé, des, dé, demos, deis, den**
Preterite indicative	**dí, diste, dió, dimos, disteis, dieron**

DECIR

Present indicative	**digo, dices, dice, decimos, decís, dicen**
Present subjunctive	**diga, digas, diga, digamos, digáis, digan**
Preterite indicative	**dije, dijiste, dijo, dijimos, dijisteis, dijeron**
Future indicative	**diré, dirás, dirá, diremos, diréis, dirán**
Conditional	**diría, dirías, diría, diríamos, diríais, dirían**
Imperative	**di** **decid**
Present participle	**diciendo**
Past participle	**dicho**

ESTAR

Present indicative	**estoy, estás, está, estamos, estáis, están**
Present subjunctive	**esté, estés, esté estemos, estéis, estén**
Preterite indicative	**estuve, estuviste, estuvo, estuvimos, estuvisteis, estuvieron**
Imperative	**está** **estad**

HABER

Present indicative	**he, has, ha, hemos, habéis, han**
Present subjunctive	**haya, hayas, haya, hayamos, hayáis, hayan**

HABER

hube, hubiste, hubo, hubimos, hubisteis, hubieron
habré, habrás, habrá, habremos, habréis, habrán
habría, habrías, habría, habríamos, habríais, habrían

HACER

...go, haces, hace, hacemos, hacéis, hacen
...ga, hagas, haga, hagamos, hagáis, hagan
...e, hiciste, hizo, hicimos, hicisteis, hicieron
...naré, harás, hará, haremos, haréis, harán

Conditional	haría, harías, haría, haríamos, haríais, harían
Imperative	haz haced
Past participle	hecho

IR

Present indicative	voy, vas, va, vamos, vais, van
Present subjunctive	vaya, vayas, vaya, vayamos, vayáis, vayan
Imperfect indicative	iba, ibas, iba, íbamos, ibais, iban
Preterite indicative	fuí, fuiste, fué, fuimos, fuisteis, fueron
Imperative	ve id
Present participle	yendo

OÍR

Present indicative	oigo, oyes, oye, oímos, oís, oyen
Present subjunctive	oiga, oigas, oiga, oigamos, oigáis, oigan
Preterite indicative	oí, oíste, oyó, oímos, oísteis, oyeron
Imperative	oye oíd
Present participle	oyendo
Past participle	oído

PODER

Preterite indicative	pude, pudiste, pudo, pudimos, pudistis, pudieron
Future indicative	podré, podrás, podrá, podremos, podréis, podrán
Conditional	podría, podrías, podría, podríamos, podríais, podrían
Present participle	pudiendo

PONER

Present indicative	pongo, pones, pone, ponemos, ponéis, ponen
Present subjunctive	ponga, pongas, ponga, pongamos, pongáis, pongan
Preterite indicative	puse, pusiste, puso, pusimos, pusisteis, pusieron
Future indicative	pondré, pondrás, pondrá, pondremos, pondréis, pondrán
Conditional	pondría, pondrías, pondría, pondríamos, pondríais, pon-
Imperative	pon poned [drían
Past participle	puesto

QUERER

Preterite indicative	quise, quisiste, quiso, quisimos, quisisteis, quisieron
Future indicative	querré, querrás, querrá, querremos, querréis, querrán
Conditional	querría, querrías, querría, querríamos, querríais, querrían

142

REÍR

Present indicative	río, ríes, ríe, reímos, reís, ríen
Present subjunctive	ría, rías, ría, ríamos, ríais, rían
Preterite indicative	reí, reíste, rió, reímos, reísteis, rieron
Imperative	ríe reíd
Present participle	riendo
Past participle	reído

SABER

Present indicative	sé, sabes, sabe, sabemos, sabéis, saben
Present subjunctive	sepa, sepas, sepa, sepamos, sepáis, sepan
Preterite indicative	supe, supiste, supo, supimos, supisteis, supieron
Future indicative	sabré, sabrás, sabrá, sabremos, sabréis, sabrán
Conditional	sabría, sabrías, sabría, sabríamos, sabríais, sabrían

SALIR

Present indicative	salgo, sales, sale, salimos, salís, salen
Present subjunctive	salga, salgas, salga, salgamos, salgáis, salgan
Future indicative	saldré, saldrás, saldrá, saldremos, saldréis, saldrán
Conditional	saldría, saldrías, saldría, saldríamos, saldríais, saldrían
Imperative	sal salid

SER

Present indicative	soy, eres, es, somos, sois, son
Present subjunctive	sea, seas, sea, semos, seáis, sean
Imperfect indicative	era, eras, era, éramos, erais, eran
Preterite indicative	fuí, fuiste, fué, fuimos, fuisteis, fueron
Imperative	sé sed

TENER

Present indicative	tengo, tienes, tiene, tenemos, tenéis, tienen
Present subjunctive	tenga, tengas, tenga, tengamos, tengáis, tengan
Preterite indicative	tuve, tuviste, tuvo, tuvimos, tuvisteis, tuvieron
Future indicative	tendré, tendrás, tendrá, tendremos, tendréis, tendrán
Conditional	tendría, tendrías, tendría, tendríamos, tendríais, tendrían
Imperative	ten tened

TRAER

Present indicative	traigo, traes, trae, traemos, traéis, traen
Present subjunctive	traiga, traigas, traiga, traigamos, traigáis, traigan
Preterite indicative	traje, trajiste, trajo, trajimos trajisteis, trajeron
Present participle	traído
Past participle	trayendo

VALER

Present indicative	valgo, vales, vale, valemos, valéis, valen
Present subjunctive	valga, valgas, valga, valgamos, valgáis, valgan
Future indicative	valdré, valdrás, valdrá, valdremos, valdréis, valdrán
Conditional	valdría, valdrías, valdría, valdríamos, valdríais, valdrían
Imperative	val(e) valed

VENIR

Present indicative	vengo, vienes, viene, venimos, venís, vienen
Present subjunctive	venga, vengas, venga, vengamos, vengáis, vengan
Preterite indicative	vine, viniste, vino, vinimos, vinisteis, vinieron
Future indicative	vendré, vendrás, vendrá, vendremos, vendréis, vendrán
Conditional	vendría, vendrías, vendría, vendríamos, vendríais, vendrían
Imperative	ven venid
Present participle	viniendo

VER

Present indicative	veo, ves, ve, vemos, veis, ven
Present subjunctive	vea, veas, vea, veamos, veáis, vean
Imperfect indicative	veía, veías, veía, veíamos, veíais, veían
Past participle	visto

WORDS SIMILAR IN ENGLISH AND SPANISH

Following is a list of Spanish words alike or almost alike in spelling, and alike in meaning in at least one acceptation to their English equivalents.

In this list of words a slight change is made in the ending of the English word to obtain the Spanish.

abrupto	agresor	Atlántico	calendario
absceso	aire	átomo	calma
absoluto	alarma	atractivo	candidato
absorbente	alarmista	autócrata	canino
abstinente	amazona	automático	canoa
abstracto	alfabeto		carácter
absurdo	altitud	bálsamo	caravana
abundante	ambulancia	banco	carbonato
abusivo	antecedente	banda	carpintero
acceso	antídoto	banquete	caso
accidente	aparte	barbarismo	católico
acento	apetito	barbero	causa
ácido	aplauso	barómetro	caverna
acróbata	apóstol	baronesa	cemento
activo	apto	bastardo	centinela
acto	archivo	bautismo	centro
adepto	argumento	bayoneta	cigarro
adjetivo	árido	Biblia	cisterna
adulterante	aristócrata	biplano	clase
adulto	arma	blando	cliente
adverbio	arrogante	bote (boat)	coexistente
adverso	asfalto	bravo	columna
aeroplano	ártico	burlesco	comandante
ágata	asalto	busto	comando
agente	aspirina		combate
agresivo	astuto	cablegrama	cometa

144

cómico	dinamita	fanático	inherente
compatriota	directo	favorito	inmenso
complemento	discordia	femenino	inmigrante
completo	discreto	festivo	inminente
complexo	disputa	figura	insolente
componente	distancia	final	instante
compromiso	distante	firme	instrumento
común	distinto	forma	insuficiente
concepto	distrito	fortuna	insulto
conciso	divino	fractura	inteligente
concreto	do(u)ble	fragante	intento
concubina	doctrina	frágil	intolerante
conducta	documento	fragmento	
conductivo	domicilio	franco	justicia
confidencia	dramático	frecuente	
conflicto		frontera	kilogramo
congreso	edicto	fruta	kilómetro
consonante	edificio	futuro	
constante	efectivo		límite
constructivo	efecto	galante	línea
contacto	egoísta	galóre	lista
contento	elástico	gangrena	lógica
continente	electivo	garantía	lotería
contrabando	electo	gasolina	
contracto	eléctrico	globo	madama
contraste	elegancia	grupo	magnitud
conveniente	elegante	guarda	mapa
convento	emigrante		marcha
convicto	eminente	hábito	margen
cooperativo	época	heraldo	marinero
correcto	etiqueta	héroe	masculino
costa	evidencia	heroísmo	matrona
credencial	evidente	humano	mayo
crédito	exacto		mérito
cresta	excelente	idea	modelo
criatura	excéntrico	idealista	moderno
crimen	excesivo	idiota	monoplano
crítico	exceso	ídolo	monte
curso	existencia	ignorante	moralista
curva	expansivo	ilegal	motor
	experiencia		música
defecto	experimento	imbécil	
demanda	experto	importante	narcótico
democrático	expresivo	incidente	negligente
demonio	exquisito	indiferente	noticia
depósito	extensivo	indirecto	novela
déspota	extinto	individual	novelista
despotismo	extracto	indulgente	novicio
diadema		infante	
diferente	falso	infinitivo	obscuro
diminutivo	famoso	infrecuente	occidente

145

océano	pretexto	romanticismo	tormento
ofensivo	problema	romántico	tráfico
orgánico	producto		tranquilo
organismo	programa	sacramento	tránsito
órgano	prostituta	sarcasmo	transparente
oriente	proverbio	secreto	triunfo
original	prudente	secta	trópico
	público	sereno	trote
pacto	pupilo	severo	tubo
paganismo	pútrido	sexo	tumulto
palacio		sincero	turbulento
palma	radiante	símbolo	turno
pánico	rancho	socialista	
parte	rápido	solemne	úlcera
patriota	rata	suma	uniforme
patriotismo	raza	sólido	union
penitente	realista	suficiente	
período	reforma	supremo	válido
persona	relativo		valiente
piloto	renta	facto	verbo
pistola	república	talento	versátil
planeta	repugnante	teléfono	verso
planta	reserva	telegrama	víctima
poema	residente	temperatura	violento
poeta	respeto	texto	violeta
pompa	restaurante	timido	violinista
portero	resto	tolerante	visita
pote	resulta	tomate	volcán
presidente	rollo	tonsilitis	zona

The following list of words ending in "tad" or "dad" in Spanish are feminine and end in "ty" in English. They are of the neuter gender in English.

absurdidad	atrocidad	claridad
aceptabilidad	austeridad	comodidad
actividad	autenticidad	compatibilidad
actualidad	autoridad	complicidad
adaptabilidad		comunidad
adversidad	barbaridad	conformidad
afabilidad	brevedad	continuidad
afinidad	brutalidad	cristiandad
agilidad		crueldad
alterabilidad	calamidad	curiosidad
animosidad	calidad	
ansiedad	cantidad	debilidad
anterioridad	capacidad	densidad
amabilidad	caridad	dificultad
ambigüedad	casualidad	dignidad
amenidad	cavidad	divinidad
antigüedad	civilidad	durabilidad

146

elasticidad	infinidad	prioridad
electricidad	informalidad	probidad
entidad	ingenuidad	probabilidad
especialidad	iniquidad	profundidad
esterilidad	inmensidad	prosperidad
eternidad	inmoralidad	proximidad
eventualidad	inmunidad	puntualidad
extremidad	integridad	
	intensidad	raridad
facilidad	irregularidad	realidad
facultad		receptabilidad
falsedad	liberalidad	regularidad
familiaridad	libertad	removibilidad
fatalidad	localidad	responsabilidad
fecundidad		
felicidad	maternidad	sagacidad
ferocidad	majestad	seguridad
fertilidad	moralidad	sensibilidad
fidelidad	multiplicidad	serenidad
flexibilidad		severidad
formalidad	nacionalidad	simplicidad
fragilidad	natividad	sinceridad
	necesidad	singularidad
generalidad	neutralidad	sociedad
generosidad		solemnidad
gravedad	obscuridad	solidaridad
	oportunidad	suavidad
habilidad		superioridad
honestidad	paternidad	
hostilidad	peculiaridad	temeridad
humanidad	personalidad	totalidad
humildad	perversidad	tranquilidad
	piedad	
identidad	pluralidad	universidad
igualdad	popularidad	utilidad
imposibilidad	porosidad	
incredulidad	posibilidad	variedad
individualidad	posteridad	velocidad

The following list of words ending in "ción" in Spanish end in "tion" in English and mean the same thing in at least one acceptation:

abducción	adoración	amputación
absolución	adulteración	animación
abstracción	adquisición	anticipación
aceptación	adulación	aplicación
acción	afección	aposición
acumulación	agitación	apropiación
acusación	agregación	arbitración
administración	alternación	argumentación
admiración	ambición	articulación

147

aserción	contracción	edición
asimilación	contradicción	educación
asociación	contribución	ejecución
aspiración	convención	elección
atención	conversación	elevación
atracción	convicción	elocución
aumentación	convocación	emancipación
autorización	cooperación	emigración
aviación	coordinación	emoción
	corporación	enumeración
calificación	corrección	equivocación
capitalización	corrupción	erudición
capitulación	creación	erupción
celebración	cristalización	estación
certificación	cultivación	estimación
circulación		estrangulación
civilización	declamación	evacuación
clasificación	declaración	evaporación
colaboración	decoración	evicción
colección	dedificación	evolución
colonización	definición	exageración
combinación	degeneración	exaltación
comparación	deliberación	excavación
compensación	demostración	excepción
competición	denominación	exclamación
complicación	deportación	exhibición
composición	deposición	expedición
comunicación	depreciación	expiración
concentración	derivación	exploración
concepción	descripción	explotación
conciliación	deserción	exportación
condenación	designación	exposición
condición	desolación	extracción
confección	destitución	extradición
confederación	destrucción	
confirmación	detención	fabricación
conflagración	determinación	facción
congratulación	detonación	fascinación
congregación	devastación	federación
conjugación	devoción	felicitación
conjunción	dirección	ficción
conmoción	discreción	formación
conservación	disipación	fortificación
consideración	disolución	fricción
constelación	disposición	fumigación
constitución	distinción	función
construcción	distracción	fundación
contaminación	distribución	
contemplación	dominación	generación
contención	duración	generalización
continuación		glorificación

148

graduación	manifestación	porción
	manipulación	posición
habitación	mediación	precaución
	meditación	precipitación
identificación	mención	predicción
iluminación	mitigación	predilección
ilustración	moción	predisposición
imaginación	moderación	premeditación
imitación	modificación	preoccupación
imperfección	mortifiación	preparación
imploración	multiplicación	preposición
importación	munición	presentación
imposición		preservación
inauguración	nación	presunción
inclinación	narración	prevaricación
indicación	natación	prevención
indignación	naturalización	privación
infección	navegación	probación
información	negación	proclamación
infracción	negociación	producción
iniciación	noción	prohibición
immigración	nominación	prolongación
inscripción	notación	promoción
insinuación	notificación	promulgación
inspección	numeración	pronunciación
inspiración	nutrición	proporción
instigación		proposición
institución	objeción	prosecución
instrucción	obligación	prostitución
insurrección	observación	protección
intención	obstrucción	provocación
interjección	ocupación	publicación
interpretación	operación	pulverización
interrogación	oposición	puntuación
intervención	oración	purificación
introducción	orientación	
invención	organización	ración
investigación	oscilación	radiación
invitación	osificación	ratificación
	ostentación	reacción
jurisdicción	ovación	realización
	oxidación	recapitulación
lamentación		recepción
legación	palpitación	reciprocación
legalización	participación	recitación
legislación	penetración	reclamación
liberación	percepción	recomendación
limitación	perfección	reconciliación
lubricación	perforación	recreación
	persecución	rectificación
mancipación	petición	reducción

149

reelección	retribución	terminación
refracción	revelación	testificación
refrigeración	reverberación	tracción
rehabilitación	revolución	tradición
relación	rotación	transacción
relegación		transición
remuneración	salutación	translación
rendición	salvación	transmigración
renovación	sanción	transportación
renunciación	satisfacción	transposición
reorganización	saturación	
reparación	sección	vacilación
repetición	selección	vaporación
representación	sensación	variación
reproducción	separación	vegetación
repudiación	significación	ventilación
reputación	simplificación	vibración
requisición	simulación	vindicación
reservación	situación	visitación
resignación	solidificación	violación
resolución	solución	vocación
respiración	subscripción	vocalización
restauración	suposición	vociferación
resurrección	substitución	volición
retención		

In the following list of words the Spanish "io" and "ia" end in "y" in English. In a few of the words listed below there is a slight change in spelling. In some instances, shown with parentheses, the English letter is omitted in the Spanish word:

academia	canario	disentería	industria
accesorio	categoría	dormitorio	infamia
adulterio	centenario		infancia
adversario	ceremonia	economía	injuria
agencia	colonia	energía	
agonía	comedia	estudio	laboratoria
analogía	comentario	extraordinario	
aniversario	comisario		matrimonio
antropología	compañía	farmacia	melodía
arbitrario	constancia	familia	memoria
armonía	contrario	fantasía	mercurio
arteria	copia	frecuencia	ministerio
artillería	coquetería	func(t)ionario	miseria
auditorio	cortesía	furia	modestia
		galantería	monasterio
		galería	monopolio
batería	depositario	geografía	
blasfemia	dinastía	gloria	observatorio
	diplomacia		oratorio
calvario	directorio	idolatría	

ordinario	plenipotenciario	salario	territorio
orgía	prodigio	san(c)tuario	testimonio
	promontorio	satisfactoria	tiranía
patrimonio	purgatorio	secretario	
pedagogía		seminario	victoria
perfidia	remedio	sociología	voluntario
perfumería	rosario	sumario	

Drop the infinitive ending in Spanish for the English verb:

abandonar	concertar	embarcar	lamentar
absorber	concurrir	emitir	limitar
abundar	conducir	enamorar	
aceptar	conferir	engendrar	manifestar
aclamar	confesar	entrar	marcar
acordar	confirmar	estampar	marchar
acreditar	conformar	exaltar	molestar
adaptar	confrontar	exclamar	murmurar
administrar	consentir	exhortar	
admitir	considerar	existir	ocasionar
adoptar	consignar	expeler	ocurrir
adornar	consistir	experimentar	ofender
aducir	consultar	exportar	omitir
afectar	contar	expresar	
afirmar	contender	extender	partir
alarmar	contentar		pasar
alterar	contrastar	filtrar	perdonar
anexar	convertir	fomentar	permitir
anular	corresponder	frecuentar	persistir
apelar	costar	func(t)ionar	perturbar
aplaudir		fundar	ponderar
aprehender	debutar		preferir
aprisionar	defender	guardar	presentar
armar	deferir		preservar
arrestar	defraudar	honrar	pretender
asaltar	demandar		proclamar
ascender	departir	importar	profesar
asentir	depender	incurrir	prolongar
asignar	deportar	inferir	proporcionar
atacar	depositar	informar	prosperar
atender	desarmar	insertar	protestar
	descender	insistir	proyectar
balancear	descontar	inspeccionar	
batallar	desembarcar	instalar	razonar
	desistir	insultar	reclamar
calmar	despachar	interesar	recomendar
cancelar	destilar	internar	recurrir
combatir	detallar	interpretar	referir
comentar	detestar	inventar	reformar
comisionar	divorciar		refrenar
concernir		laborar	registrar

151

remitir	retardar	sufrir	transportar
repetir	robar	sumar	triunfar
rescindir		suspender	
responder	salvar		usurpar
representar	sanc(t)ionar	telefonear	
resignar	solicitar	tostar	vender
resistir	soportar	transformar	visitar
respetar	subsistir	transmitir	vomitar
resultar	sucumbir		

In this list of words the Spanish infinitive is replaced by a silent "e" in English. Some of these words have slight changes in spelling. English double letters are single in Spanish. Soft "c" before "a" or "o" is changed to "z." The "dv" combination in many English words changes to "v" in Spanish.

abjurar	combinar	determina	implorar
absolver	comenzar	dilatar	improvisar
abusar	comparar	dispensar	incitar
acceder	competir	dispersar	inclinar
acreditar	completar	dividir	inducir
acusar	computar	divulgar	inflamar
admirar	conceder	do(u)blar	inquirir
adorar	condensar		inspirar
adherir	confinar	economizar	intervenir
adquirir	conjurar	eclipsar	introducir
aludir	consolar	eludir	invadir
analizar	conspirar	equipar	invitar
aprobar	consumir	escalar	invocar
argüir	continuar	escandalizar	
aspirar	convencer	escapar(se)	mover
asumir	conversar	evadir	
autorizar	curar	evocar	notar
avanzar		examinar	
a(d)vanzar	danzar	exceder	
aventurar	datar	excitar	obligar
a(d)venturar	decidir	excusar	observar
a(d)visar	declarar	exhalar	opinar
	declinar	expirar	organizar
basar	deducir	explorar	
	definir	expulsar	paralizar
capitalizar	defraudar		perfumar
capturar	denotar	fatigar	persuadir
caracterizar	denunciar	figurar	practicar
carbonizar	deplorar	forzar	preparar
causar	depravar	fracturar	preseverar
censurar	describir		presidir
citar	desfigurar	ignorar	presumir
civilizar	desolver	imaginar	procurar
coincidir	destinar	impedir	producir

152

profanar	reducir	resolver	servir
pronunciar	refinar	respirar	subscribir
proscribir	relatar	resumir	
provocar	remover	retirar	tranquilizar
pulverizar	renunciar	revocar	tributar
	reparar	revolver	
realizar	repasar		
recibir	reposar	saludar	usar
reclinar	reproducir	seducir	utilizar
recompensar	reservar	sentenciar	
redo(u)blar	residir	separar	votar

The following verbs end in "ar" in Spanish and in "ate" in English:

abdicar	congregar	emancipar	investigar
abreviar	conjugar	emigrar	irritar
abrogar	commemorar	enumerar	
acelerar	consolidar	enunciar	libertar
acentuar	consumar	especificar	lubricar
acomoddar	contaminar	estimar	
actuar	contemplar	evacuar	manipular
acumular	cooperar	exagerar	mediar
adulterar	coordinar	excavar	meditar
agitar	crear	exterminar	mitigar
aglomerar	cultivar		moderar
agravar		facilitar	modular
agregar	debilitar	fascinar	motivar
aliviar	decorar	felicitar	mutilar
alternar	dedicar	formular	
amputar	degenerar	fluctuar	narrar
animar	delegar		navegar
anotar	deliberar	graduar	necesitar
anticipar	demo(n)strar	granular	negociar
apreciar	denominar		nominar
aprop(r)iar	depredar	habilitar	obligar
arbitrar	designar	habitar	oficiar
articular	desolar	habituar	operar
asesinar	devastar		orientar
	dictar	iluminar	originar
calcular	diferenciar	ilustrar	oscilar
calumniar	dilatar	implicar	
castigar	disimular	inaugurar	palpitar
castrar	disipar	incorporar	participar
celebrar	dislocar	indicar	penetrar
circular	dominar	iniciar	perpetuar
complicar	donar	inocular	precipitar
comunicar	duplicar	insinular	predominar
concentrar		instigar	premeditar
conciliar	educar	interrogar	promulgar
confiscar	elevar	intimar	propagar
congratular	emanar	invalidar	pun(c)tuar

153

radiar	remunerar	sofocar	vacilar
reanimar	renovar	subyugar	vegetar
recapitular	renunciar	suplicar	venerar
reciprocar	resucitar		ventilar
recrear		terminar	vibrar
refrigerar	saturar	tolerar	
regenerar	separar	transmigrar	vindicar
reiterar	simular		violar
relegar	situar	ulcerar	vociferar

Below is given a list of words that are spelled alike (or almost alike) in Spanish and English and mean the same thing in at least one acceptation:

abdomen	auto	colisión	déficit
abominable	automóvil	colonial	depresión
abrasión	aversión	color	derivable
accesible	aviador	comercial	detestable
accidental	axioma	comisión	detector
acre		comparable	diagnosis
actor	balance	compulsión	difusión
actual	bulevar	concesión	digestible
admirable	bonanza	conclusión	digestión
adobe	brutal	cóndor	dimensión
adorable	billón	confesión	director
adverbial		confusión	dirigible
agresión	cable	considerable	diván
agresor	calibre	cónsul	diversión
álbum	calicó	consular	división
álcali	calomel	continental	doctor
alcohol	canal	convoy	dogma
alfalfa	cáncer	corral	dorsal
altar	candor	cordial	dragón
alusión	caníbal	corporal	drama
aluvial	cañón	coyote	
amén	canon	cráter	eczema
ángel	capital	criminal	editorial
angular	cardinal	crisis	elector
animal	carnal	cristal	electorial
antena	cartel	cruel	elemental
anterior	casual	cuestión	era
anual	celestial	culpable	error
apendicitis	censor	curable	especial
aplicable	central	champaña	estimable
área	cereal	charlatán	etcétera
arena	chocolate	chasis	evasión
armada	circular		excursión
artificial	civil	deán	experimental
ascensión	clamor	debate	explosión
atlas	clerical	decimal	expresión
audible	clímax	decisión	expulsión

154

extensión	imperial	lamentable	notable
exterior	impersonal	lateral	numeral
	implacable	latín	
facial	imposible	laudable	oasis
factor	impresión	laurel	ocasión
familiar	incomparable	legal	ocasional
fatal	incompatible	legión	occidental
favor	incomprehensible	liberal	omisión
favorable	incurable	local	oficial
federal	indigestión	lustre	ómnibus
felón	indispensable		ópera
fértil	indisputable	magnate	opinión
fervor	individual	magneto	ordinal
fiasco	indivisible	maíz	oriental
filial	industrial	mamá	oral
final	inestimable	mansión	origen
flexible	inevitable	manual	original
formal	infalible	marginal	ornamental
formidable	inferior	marital	
fórmula	infernal	material	panorama
fraternal	inflamable	maternal	par
fundamental	informal	melón	particular
funeral	inimitable	memorable	pasión
	innumerable	memorial	pastoral
galón	insensible	mental	paternal
gas	inseparable	metal	peculiar
general	inspector	mineral	pedestal
genial	instructor	miserable	penal
glacial	instrumental	misión	península
gonorrea	insuperable	moral	peninsular
gorila	integral	mormón	pensión
gradual	intelectual	mortal	peón
gratis	inteligible	mosquito	perfume
guardián	interior	motor	perpendicular
	interminable	mulato	personal
habitual	intolerable	múltiple	piano
hangar	intrusión	municipal	pistón
honor	invariable	mural	placer
horrible	invasión	musical	plan
horizontal	inventor		plural
horror	invisible	natal	polar
hospital	irregular	natural	popular
hotel	irremediable	naval	portal
humor	irresistible	negociable	posible
		negro	postal
idea	jovial	neuralgia	posterior
ideal	judicial	neutral	practicable
ilusión		no	preceptor
imaginable	kodak	noble	precisión
imitable		nominal	prior
imperceptible	labor	normal	probable

155

profesional	revisión	sublime	ulterior
promotor	revocable	sultán	unión
propaganda	revólver	superficial	universal
provincial	rifle	superior	usual
provisional	rigor	suspensión	
provisión	ritual		vapor
pulmotor	romance	tango	variable
pus	rufián	temporal	venerable
	rumor	tenis	
radial	rural	tenor	verbal
radiar		tensión	versión
radical	salón	terrible	vertical
radio	secular	terror	viceversa
rebelión	sensible	tolerable	vigor
rector	sentimental	total	violín
región	separable	tractor	virginal
regular	sexual	transferible	virtual
religión	similar	tribunal	visible
remediable	simple	trío	visión
reparable	singular	triple	visual
repulsión	social	trivial	vital
resistible	sofá	tropical	vocal
restaurant	soluble	tumor	vulgar
reversible	suave	tutor	

The following list of words ending in "ista" in Spanish refers to one who is of that occupation or member of the group.

The word is masculine or feminine according to the gender of the person.

absolutista	capitalista	maquinista
adornista	comunista	moralista
agrarista	comisionista	motorista
alarmista	conformista	
alienista	contrabandista	naturalista
alquimista		novelista
analista	dentista	
anarquista	droguista	
antagonista	duelista	oculista
archivista		
artista	economista	pianista
automovilista	electricista	protagonista
bañista	fatalista	realista
bautista		
biciclista	huelgista	socialista
bimetalista		
bolchevista	idealista	violinista

THE STATES OF MEXICO AND THEIR ABBREVIATIONS

Aguascalientes—Ags.
Baja California—B. C.
Campeche—Camp.
Chiapas—Chis.
Chihuahua—Chih.
Coahuila—Coah.
Colima—Col.
Distrito Federal—D. F.
Durango—Dgo.
Guanajuato—Gto.
Guerrero—Gro.
Hidalgo—Hgo.
Jalisco—Jal.
México—Mex.
Michoacán—Mich.
Morelos—Mor.

Nayarit—Nay.
Nuevo León—N. L.
Oaxaca—Oax.
Puebla—Pueb.
Querétaro—Qto.
Quintana Roo (no abbreviation)
San Luis Potosí—S. L. P.
Sinaloa—Sin.
Sonora—Son.
Tabasco—Tab.
Tamaulipas—Tamps.
Tlaxcala—Tlax.
Veracruz—Ver.
Yucatán—Yuc.
Zacatecas—Zac.

OCCUPATIONS

agent—agente
artist—artista
aviator—aviador
ballplayer—pelotero
barber—peluquero
   barbero
blacksmith—herrero
bookkeeper—tenedor de libros
book seller—librero
bootblack—limpiabotas, bolero
butcher—carnicero
carpenter—carpintero
cattleman—ganadero
chauffeur—chofer, chófer
chicken raiser—gallinero
clerk—dependiente
conductor—conductor
constable—alguacil
cook—cocinero
cotton grower—algodonero
cowboy—vaquero
customs agent—agente de aduana
   aduanero
dairyman—lechero
dancer—bailador
   bailarina
dentist—dentista
director—director
doctor—doctor
   médico

driver—muletero (horses)
   cochero (coach)
druggist—boticario
   droguista
   droguero
engineer—ingeniero
farmer—hacendado
   agricultor
fisherman—pescador
gardener—jardinero
goatherd—chivero
   cabrero
guide—guía
harvester—cosechero
hatmaker—sombrerero
inventor—inventor
irrigator—regador
jeweler—joyero
laborer—jornalero
   trabajador
   labrador
lawyer—abogado
   licenciado
machinist—maquinista
mailcarrier—cartero
manufacturer—fabricante
mason—albañil
merchant—comerciante
mechanic—mecánico
midwife—partera

miller—**molinero**	seamstress—**costurera**
miner—**minero**	sharecropper—**mediero**
musician—**músico**	shepherd—**pastor**
nurse—**enfermera**	**borreguero**
obstetrician—**partero**	sheriff—**alguacil**
official—**oficial**	**policía**
painter—**pintor**	shoemaker—**zapatero**
peddler—**comerciante ambulante**	soldier—**soldado**
buhonero	stenographer—**taquígrafo**
picker (cotton)—**piscador**	surgeon—**cirujano**
pilot—**piloto**	swineherd—**porquero**
plasterer—**emplastador**	tailor—**sastre**
plumber—**plomero**	teacher—**profesor**
planter—**plantador**	**maestro**
sembrador	tinsmith—**hojalatero**
porter—**portero**	usher—**conserje, acomodador**
cargador	valet—**camarero**
priest—**cura**	waiter—**mozo, mesero**
promoter—**promotor**	washerwoman—**lavandera**
rancher—**ranchero**	watchmaker—**relojero**
sailor—**marinero**	woodchopper—**leñero**
seller—**vendedor**	woodworker (cabinetmaker)—**ebanista**
servant—**mozo**	worker—**trabajador**
sirviente	**obrero**
criado	

SPANISH-ENGLISH VOCABULARY[26]

a—to, at
abajo—under, below, down
abandonado—abandoned
abierto—opened
abril, m—April
abrir—to open
abuela, f—grandmother
abuelo, m—grandfather
acá—here
acabar—to end, finish
acercarse—to approach, come near
acompañar—to accompany
adelante—ahead, forward
aflojar—to relax, loosen
agosto, m—August
agua, f (el)—water
ahí—there (by you)
ahora—now
ahorita—right now
al—to the, at the

alambre, m—wire
albañil, m—bricklayer
al fin—at least, finally
alemán, a—German
algo—something
algodón, m—cotton
alguien—somebody
alguna vez—ever, sometime
alguno—some
alimento, m—food
almacén, m—wholesale house
alto—tall, high, halt
alumno(a)—pupil, student
allá—there, over yonder
allí—there
amanecer, m—dawn (to dawn)
amarillo—yellow
americano(a)—American
amigo(a)—friend
andar—to walk

[26] Radical changing verbs are listed with the Roman numerals, (I), (II), (III), placed after the infinitive according to their classification.

anillo, m—ring
Anita—Annie
anoche—last night
anochecer—to grow dark
anteanoche—night before last
anteayer—day before yesterday
anterior—preceding, former
antes—before (adv.)
antes de—before (prep.)
año, m—year
año nuevo, m—New Year
aquí—here
aprender—to learn
arado, m—plow
archivar—to file
archivo, m—file, archive
arrestar—to arrest
asiento, m—seat
asiento de atrás—back seat
asiento de enfrente—front seat
atrás—behind, back, past
aunque—although
aun—ever, still, yet, as yet
auto, m—auto, car
automóvil, m—automobile
ave, f—fowl
avenida, f—avenue
ayer—yesterday
ayudar—to help
azul—blue

baile, m—dance
bajar—to lower, get down
bajo—low, short, underneath
bastante—enough
bastar—to be enough
beber—to drink
bien—well
blanco—white
blanquillo, m—egg
bonito—pretty
bote, m—boat
botella, f—bottle
brincar—to jump
bueno—good
buque, m—ship
buscar—to look for

caballo, m—horse
cabello, m—hair
caber—to contain, fit into

cada—each, every
caer—to fall
café—brown, coffee, café
caliente—warm
calle, f—street
caminar—to travel
camino, m—road
camisa, f—shirt
campo, m—country, field
cansado—tired
cantina, f—saloon
capitación, f—headtax
carga, f—load, freight, cargo
cárcel, f—jail
Carlos, f—Charles
carretera, f—highway
carro, m—car, auto
carta, f—letter
casa, f—house
cazar—to hunt
cerca, f—fence
cerca (adv.)—near
cerca de (prep.)—near
certificado, m—certificate
cerveza, f—beer
chaqueta, f—jacket
chivo, m—goat
chocar—to collide
chofer, m—chauffeur, driver
choque, m—wreck
cicatriz, f—scar
cine, m—picture show, movie
ciudad, f—city
ciudadanía, f—citizenship
ciudadano(a)—citizen
cita, f—date, engagement
cierto—certain
claramente—clearly
claro—clear
cobija, f—blanket
cobrar—to collect, charge
coche, m—car, coach
cócono, m—turkey
codorniz, f—quail
colocar—to place
color, m—color
comer—to eat
comerciante, m—merchant
comida, f—dinner, food
comisionista, m—commission merchant
como—as, like

159

¿cómo?—how?
compañero(a)—companion
compañía, f—company
compartimiento, m—compartment
comprar—to buy
con—with
condado, m—county
conducir—to conduct, lead
conejo, m—rabbit
conmigo—with me
conocer—to be acquainted with
conocido(a)—acquaintance
conseguir (III)—to get, obtain
cónsul, m—consul
consulado, m—consulate
construir—to construct
contento—contented
contestar—to answer
contigo—with you (fam.)
contrabandista, m—smuggler
corbata, f—necktie
correo, m—postoffice, mail
corto—short
cosa, f—thing
cosecha, f—harvest
cosechar—to harvest
coyote, m—coyote
creer—to believe, think
crema, f—cream
criar—to raise
cruz, f—cross
cruzar—to cross
¿cuál?—which?
¿cuándo?—when?
¿cuánto?—how much?
¿cuántos?—how many?
cuarto, m—room, quarter, fourth
cuenta, f—bill
cuero, m—leather
cuidado—care
cuidadosamente—carefully
cumpleaños, m—birthday
curva, f—curve

dar—to give
de—of, from
debajo (adv.)—under, beneath
debajo de (prep.)—under, beneath
decir—to say, tell
dedo, m—finger
delante (adv.)—before, ahead, in front

delante de (prep.)—before, ahead of, in front of
delantero—front
dentro—within, inside
demasiado (adv.)—too, too much
demasiado (adj.)—too much
demasiados (adj.)—too many
deportar—to deport
deporte, m—sport
deportivo—sporting
derecho—right, straight
desahijar—to thin (chop cotton), to wean
descripción, f—description
desde—since, from
desear—to desire
desidia, f—laziness, indolence
desierto, m—desert
despedir (III)—to dismiss, discharge
despedirse (III)—to say good-bye
después (adv.)—after, next, then
después de (prep.)—after
después que—after
detener—to stop, detain
detrás (adv.)—behind, after, back
detrás de (prep.)—behind, after, back
devolver (I)—to return, pay back
día, m—day (hoy—today)
día de fiesta—holiday
día festivo—holiday
día de descanso—day of rest
día de Navidad—Christmas
día de trabajo—work day
diario, m—daily, newspaper
diciembre, m—December
difícil—difficult
dinero, m—money
divisoria—divisional
doctor, m—doctor
dólar, m—dollar
doméstico—domestic
domingo, m—Sunday
¿dónde?—where
¿en dónde?—(in) where?
¿adónde?—(to) where?
¿de dónde?—from where? of where?
¿para dónde?—(for) where?
¿por dónde?—(through) where?
dueño, m—owner
durante—during
durar—to last

duro—hard

edad, f—age
edificio, m—building
Eduardo—Edward
ejercicio, m—exercise
emplear—to employ
empleo, m—work, employment
empleado, m—employee
empleado (adj.)—employed
en—in, on
encontrar (I)—to meet, find
enero, m—January
enfermo—sick
Enrique—Henry
enseñar—to teach, show
enterrar (I)—to bury
entonces—then
entrada, f—entry, entrance
entrar—to enter
entre—between, among
entregar—to hand, deliver
enviar—to send
envolver (I)—to wrap, bundle
escaparse—to escape
esconder—to hide
escribir—to write
escrito—written
escuchar—to listen
escuela, f—school
español, m—Spaniard
español, m—Spanish
esposa, f—wife
esposo, m—husband
estación, f—season, station
estado, m—state, status
Estados Unidos (los EE. UU.)—the United States
estar—to be
esta (adj.)—this
este, m—east
este (adj.)—this
estudiante, m-f—student
examinar—to examine
excitado—excited
extranjero, m—stranger, foreigner

fácil—easy
faltar—to lack, need
familia, f—family
febrero, m—February

fecha, f—date (time)
federal, m—federal, officer
feliz—happy
ferrocarril, m—railroad
fijarse en—to notice
firmar—to sign
freno, m—brakes, bridle
fuego, m—fire
fuera—outside
frío, m—cold (noun)
frío—cold (adj.)
furgón, m—boxcar

gallina, f—hen, chicken
ganar—to earn, win
garita, f—sentry box (entrance gate—Mexican Border)
gastar—to spend
gato, m—cat
gente, f—people
grande—large
gris—gray
guajalote, m—turkey
guiar—to guide, drive
gustar—to like, please

haber—to have (auxiliary)
hablar—to talk, speak
hacendado, m—farmer
hacer—to do, make
hacienda, f—farm
hay—there is, are
hallar—to find
hasta—until
hermana, f—sister
hermano, m—brother
hermoso—beautiful, pretty
hijo, m—son
hija, f—daughter
hombre, m—man
hora, f—hour
hotel, m—hotel
hoy—today
hoyo, m—hole (fence)
huellas, f—tracks, prints
huevo, m—egg

identificación, f—identification
iglesia, f—church
ilegal—illegal
importante—important

imposible—impossible
impresión, f—impression, print
inglés, m—English
inglesa, f—Englishwoman
inmigración, f—immigration
inspector, m—inspector
internacional—international
íntimo—intimate
invierno, m—winter
ir—to go
irse—to go away
izquierdo—left

Jorge—George
joven (adj.)—young
joven (m-f)—young person
jornalero, m—laborer
jamás—never, ever
Juan—John
jueves, m—Thursday
julio, m—July
junio, m—June
jurar—to swear (oath)

labor, f—labor, field
lado, m—side
ladrillo, m—brick
lana, f—wool
lápiz, m—pencil
largo—long
lavar—to wash
lavarse—to wash oneself
lección, f—lesson
leche, f—milk
leer—to read
legal—legal
legalmente—legally
legumbre, f—vegetable
lejos—far
lento—slow
lentamente—slowly
leña, f—firewood
libertar—to free, liberate
liebre, f—jackrabbit
límite, m—limit
limpio—clean
lindo—pretty
libro, m—book
línea, f—line
local—local
lugar, m—place

lumbre, f—fire
luna, f—moon
lunar, m—mole (on person)
lunes, m—Monday
luz, f—light
llamar—to call
llamarse—to be named
llanta, f—tire
llegada, f—arrival
llegar—to arrive
llevar—to carry, wear

madre, f—mother
madrugada, f—dawn, early morning
maíz, m—corn
mal—badly
maleta, f—suitcase
malo—bad, sick
mamá—mamma
mandar—to order, send
manejar—to drive
mano, f—hand
mantequilla, f—butter
manzana, f—apple (block, around the block)
mañana, f—morning, tomorrow
máquina, f—machine
maquinaria, f—machinery
marcar—to mark
María—Mary
marido, m—husband
marrano(a)—hog
martes, m—Tuesday
marzo, m—March
más—more
mayo—May
médico, m—doctor
medio—middle, half
mexicano, mejicano—Mexican
México, Méjico—Mexico
mejor—better
menos—less, minus
mes, m—month
mesa, f—table, plateau
metal, m—metal
meter—to put in
mientras—while
miércoles, m—Wednesday
milla, f—mile
milpa, f—maize land, cornfield
mina, f—mine

minero, m—miner
minuto, m—minute
mirada, f—glance
montar—to mount
monte, m—brush
morir (II)—to die
mostrar (I)—to show
motor, m—motor
muchacha, f—girl
muchacho, m—boy
mucho (adj. or adv.)—much
muchos (adj.)—many
muebles, m—furniture
mujer, f—woman
mula, f—mule
muy—very

nacer—to be born
nacimiento, m—birth
nacionalidad, f—nationality
nada—nothing
nadar—to swim
nadie—nobody
negocio, m—business
negro—black
ni—neither, nor
ni . . . . ni—neither . . . . nor
ninguno—none
niño(a)—child
no—no, not
noche, f—night
Nochebuena, f—Christmas Eve
nombre, m—name
norte, m—north
noviembre, m—November
número, m—number

obtener—to obtain, get
octubre, m—October
ocupado—busy
ocurrir—to occur
oeste, m—west
ofensa, f—offense
oficial, m—official
oficina, f—office
oír—to hear
oro, m—gold
otoño, m—autumn
otro—another

padre—father

pagar—to pay
país, m—country
paja, f—straw
paloma, f—dove
papá, m—papa, father
para—for, in order to
parar—to stop
parecer—to seem, appear
pared, f—wall
pasaje, m—passage
pasar—to pass
pasar—to spend (time)
paso, m—pass, step
pato, m—duck
patrón, m—boss
pedir (III)—to ask for
película, f—film
pelo, m—hair
pelota, f—ball
pensar (I)—to think, intend
peor—worse
pequeño—small
perder (I)—to lose
perezoso—lazy (lazy—flojo, more common)
periódico, m—newspaper
permiso, m—permit, permission
pero—but
persona, f—person
peso, m—dollar (Mexican)
pie, m—foot
piel, f—skin, hide
piscar—to pick
pistola, f—pistol
planchar—to iron, press
plantar—to plant
plata, f—silver
platicar—to chat
plato, m—plate, dish
plaza, f—plaza, square
pluma, f—pen
pobre—poor
poco (adj)—little
pocos (adj.)—few
poder (I)—to be able, can
pollo, m—chicken, fryer
poner—to put, place
ponerse—to put on
por—for, through, by
por eso—for that reason
porque—because

¿por qué?—why?
portero, m—porter
posible—possible
preparar—to prepare
presentar—to present
primavera, f—spring
primo(a)—cousin
promesa, f—promise
prometer—to promise
próximo—next
prueba, f—proof
pueblo, m—town, people
puente, m—bridge
puerco, m—hog
puerta, f—door
puerto, m—port
pues—well, then
pugada, f—inch
pugar, m—thumb

¿qué?—what?
que—that
que—(in comparisons)
¿quién?—who?
¿a quién?—whom?
¿de quién?—whose?
quedar(se)—to remain, stay
querer—to wish, want
queso, m—cheese

rápidamente—rapidly
rápido—rapid, fast
ranchero, m—rancher
rancho, m—ranch, farm
rata, f—rat
ratito, m—very short time
rato, m—short time
ratón, m—mouse
rayado—striped
recibir—to receive
recibo, m—receipt
record, m—record
registrar—to search, register
regresar—to return
renovar (I)—to renew
renta, f—rent
rentar—to rent
reparo, m—repair
retrato, m—picture
reunir—to unite, join
revelar—to reveal

revólver, m—revolver (noun)
rico—rich
río, m—river
rojo—red
ropa, f—clothes

sábado, m—Saturday
saber—to know (how)
sacar—to take out
saco, m—coat
salchichas, f—sausage
salida, f—departure
salir—to leave, depart
salud, f—health
seda, f—silk
según—according to
seguro—sure, certain, safe
semana, f—week
senda, f—path, footpath
sendero, m—path, trail
sentado—seated
sentarse (I)—to sit down
sentir (II)—to feel
señor, m—sir, Mr.
señora—Mrs.
señorita—Miss, young lady
septiembre, m—September
sepultar—to bury
si—if
sí—yes
siempre—always
siglo, m—century
signo, m—sign
silla, f—chair
silvestre—wild
sin—without
sino—but, except, only
sitio, m—site, place
solicitar—to solicit, induce
solo—alone
sólo—only
sombrero, m—hat
subir—to climb
sucio—dirty
suegra, f—mother-in-law
suegro, m—father-in-law
suerte, f—luck
sur, m—south

también—also, too, as well
tan—as, so

tampoco—neither, not either
tanto—as much
tantos—as many
tarde, f—afternoon
tarde—late
tarjeta, f—card
taxi, m—taxi
taza, f—cup
teatro, m—theater
Tejas—Texas
teléfono, m—telephone
telefonear—to telephone
temprano—early
tener—to have, possess
tequila, m—tequila
tiempo, m—time, weather
tienda, f—store
tinta, f—ink
tía, f—aunt
tío, m—uncle
tirar—to pull, shoot
todavía—yet, still
todavía no—not yet
todo—all
todo el mundo—everybody
tomar—to take, drink
Tomás—Thomas
trabajar—to work
trabajo, m—work
traer—to bring
traje, m—suit (of clothes)
trasquilar—to shear
triste—sad
tren, m—train

últimamente—lately, lastly
último—last
útil—useful

vaca, f—cow
vagón, m—wagon

valer—to be worth
válido—valid
vapor, m—ship, steam
vaquero, m—cowboy
varios(as)—several, various
vaso, m—glass
venado, m—deer
vecino(a)—neighbor
vender—to sell
venida, f—arrival, coming
venir—to come
ventana, f—window
ver—to see (visto, p.p.)
verano, m—summer
verdad, f—truth, true
verde—green
verduras, f—greens, vegetables
vestido, m—dress
vestir(se) (III)—to dress
vez, f—time (numerically)
viajar—to travel
viaje, m—trip, journey
viejo—old, old person
viernes, m—Friday
vino, m—wine
visa, f—visa
visita, f—visit
vista, f—sight, view
vivir—to live
volante—flying
voluntariamente—voluntarily

y—and
ya—already
yarda, m, f—yard
yo—I

zapatería, f—shoe shop
zapatero, m—cobbler
zapato, m—shoe
zorro, m—fox

ENGLISH-SPANISH VOCABULARY[27]

a—un, una
abandon—abandonar, dejar
able—poder (I)
about—acerca de, como

above—sobre, encima, arriba
absence—ausencia, f
absent—ausente
abuse—maltratar

[27] Words used in a slightly different meaning from the usual interpretation are indicated by an °.

165

accept—aceptar
accompany—acompañar
accord—acuerdo, m
according to—según
accuse—acusar
ache—dolor, m; doler (I)
acquaintance—conocido
acre—acre, m
across—a través de
address—dirección, f
admission—admisión, f
admit—admitir
adopt—adoptar
advice—consejo, m; aviso, m
advise—aconsejar, avisar
affair—asunto, m; negocio, m
affidavit—declaración, f
afoot—a pie
after—después (de) (que)
after—detrás de
afternoon—tarde, f
afterwards—después
again—otra vez, de nuevo
against—contra
age—edad, f
agent—agente, m
agree—convenir, estar, conforme
agreement—acuerdo, m; pacto, m
air—aire, m
alien—ajeno, m; extranjero, m
all—todo
alley—callejón, m
allow—permitir, dejar
almost—casi
alone—solo
along—a lo largo de
already—ya
also—también
although—aunque
always—siempre
America—América, f
American—americano (adj. or noun)
among—entre
an—un, una
and—y
angry—enojado
animal—animal, m
Annie—Anita
another—otro
answer—contestar, responder
any—alguno

anybody—alguien
anything—algo, alguna cosa
apartment—apartamiento, m
appear—aparecer, parecer
apple—manzana, f
application—aplicación, f
apply—aplicar, solicitar
appointment—compromiso, m; cita, f
apprehend—aprehender, arrestar,
    prender, agarrar°
approach—acercarse a
April—abril
argue—disputar, argüir
arm—brazo, m; arma, f
army—ejército, m
around—alrededor
arrange—arreglar
arrangements—arreglos, m
arrest—arrestar, arresto, m; aprehender
arrival—llegada, f; venida, f
arrive—llegar
archive—archivo, m
Arthur—Arturo
artist—artista, m
as—como
as . . . as—tan . . . como
as much . . . as—tanto . . . como
as many . . . as—tantos . . . como
ask (question)—preguntar
ask for—pedir (III)
assault—asaltar; asalto, m
assist—ayudar, asistir
assistant—ayudante, m
at—a, en
at last—al fin, por fin, finalmente
at least—al menos, por lo menos, a lo
    menos
at once—al instante, en seguida
at present—actualmente
August—agosto, m
aunt—tía, f
authorize—autorizar
automobile—automóvil, m; coche, m;
    carro, m
autumn—otoño, m
avenue—avenida, f
await—aguardar, esperar
awake—despertar (I)

baby—niño(a); bebi; nene, m; nena, f;
    infante, m

bachelor—soltero, m
back—espalda, f; atrás; detrás
back of—detrás de
bacon—tocino, m
bad—malo
badge—insignia, f; placa, f
badly—mal
baggage—equipaje, m
bail—fianza, f
baker—panadero, m
bakery—panadería, f
bald—calvo, pelón
ball—pelota, f; bola, f
bank—banco, m; barranca, f
banker—banquero, m
baptize—bautizar
baptismal certificate—fe de bautismo
bar—cantina, f
bartender—cantinero, m
barber—barbero, m; peluquero, m
barber shop—barbería, f; peluquería, f
bath—baño, m
bathe—bañarse
battery—batería, f
be—ser, estar
be able—poder (I)
be acquainted with—conocer
be born—nacer
be named—llamarse
be pleasing to—gustar
be worth—valer
beans—frijoles, m
beard—barba, f
beautiful—hermoso, lindo, bello
bed—cama, f
bedroll—mochila, f; tendido° m
because—porque
because of—a causa de, por
beer—cerveza, f
before (front of)—delante de
before (time)—antes de
beets—betabeles, m
beggar—mendigo, m; limosnero, m
begin—empezar (I), comenzar (I),
   principiar
behave—portarse
behind—atrás, detrás
believe—creer
believe in—aprobar (I)
belly—panza, f; panzón, m
belong to—pertenecer

below—abajo, bajo, debajo de
beneath—debajo, bajo
best—mejor
better—mejor
between—entre
big—grande
bigamist—bígamo, m
bigamy—bigamia, f
bird—pájaro, m
bill—cuenta, f
birth—nacimiento, m
birth certificate—certificado de nacimiento, m
birthday—cumpleaños, m
birth mark—marca de nacimiento
black—negro
blackish—prieto
blame—culpa, f
blanket—cobija, f; frazada, f
blind—ciego
block—bloque, m; cuadra, f
block—manzana, f
blond—huero, rubio
blood—sangre, f
blue—azul
boat—bote, m; buque, m; barco, m
boat (row)—chalupa, f
body—cuerpo, m
bond (bail)—fianza, f
bone—hueso, m
book—libro, m
boot—bota, f
border—frontera
Border Patrol—Patrulla de la Frontera, Patrulla Fronteriza
born—nacer, nacido
borrow—pedir (III), prestado
boss—patrón, m; mayordomo, m; jefe,
   m
boss (main)—mero gallo°
both—ambos, los dos
bottle—botella, f
boy—muchacho, m
box—caja, f
brakes—frenos, m
branch—rama, f
brawl—barulla, f; disputa, f
bread—pan, m
break into—escalar
break—quebrar, romper
breaking and entering—escalo, m

167

breakfast—**desayunar, desayuno, m**
breast—**pecho, m**
brewery—**cervecería, f**
brick—**ladrillo, m**
bricklayer—**albañil, m; ladrillero, m**
bridge—**puente, m or f**
bridle—**freno, m**
bring—**traer**
broad—**ancho**
broken—**roto, quebrado**
broom—**escoba, f**
brother—**hermano, m**
brother-in-law—**cuñado, m**
brown—**café, moreno, pardo**
brunette—**trigueño, moreno**
brush—**chaparral, m; monte, m**
brush—**matorral, m**
bucket—**balde, m; bote, m**
build—**construir**
building—**edificio, m**
bull—**toro, m**
bullet—**bala, f; balazo, m**
bundle—**bulto, m; paquete, m**
burro—**burro, m**
bury—**sepultar, enterrar (I)**
bus—**camión, m; esteche, m; bus, m;**
  ómnibus, m
business—**negocio, m; asunto, m**
busy—**ocupado**
but—**pero, sino, mas**
butcher—**carnicero, m**
butcher shop—**carnicería, f**
butter—**mantequilla, f**
button—**botón, m**
buy—**comprar**
by—**por**
by (near)—**cerca**
by means of—**por medio de**

cabbage—**col, m; repollo, m**
café—**café, m**
calf—**becerro, m; ternero, m**
call—**llamar**
can—**lata, f; bote, m**
can (to be able)—**poder (I)**
canoe—**canoa, f; chalupa, f**
cap—**cachucha, f; gorra, f**
capital—**capital, f**
car—**carro°, m; coche, m; auto, m;**
  máquina, f°; automóvil, m
car (box)—**furgón, m**

car jack—**gato, m; yaque, m**
card—**tarjeta, f**
care (to take)—**cuidar**
care—**cuidado, m**
carefully—**cuidadosamente**
carpenter—**carpintero, m**
carpenter shop—**carpintería, f**
carry—**llevar**
cash—**al contado**
cashier—**cajero, m; contador, m**
cat—**gato, m**
catch—**coger, agarrar**
cattle—**ganado, m**
cattleman—**ganadero, m**
cause—**causa, f; causar**
cemetery—**cementerio, m; patheón, m**
cent—**centavo, m**
century—**ciglo, m**
certain—**cierto, seguro**
certainly—**ciertamente; ¿cómo no?**
certificate—**certificado, m**
certify—**certificar, afirmar**
chair—**silla, f**
chalk—**tiza, f**
chance—**oportunidad, f; chanza, f**
change—**cambiar, cambio, m; mudar**
Charles—**Carlos**
charming—**simpático**
chat—**platicar, charlar**
chauffeur—**chofer, m; chófer, m**
cheap—**barato**
check—**revisar, checar**
check (commercial)—**cheque, m**
cheek—**mejilla, f**
chief—**jefe, m**
child—**niño(a), chamaco(a), criatura, f**
children—**niños, m**
chin—**barba, f; barbilla, f**
chop (cotton)—**desahijar; limpiar**
Christmas—**Navidad, f; Natividad, f**
Christmas Eve—**Nochebuena, f**
church—**iglesia, f**
cigar—**puro, m**
cigarette—**cigarro, m; cigarillo, m**
citizen—**ciudadano(a)**
citizenship—**ciudadanía, f**
city—**ciudad, f**
civil—**civil**
class—**clase, f**
clean—**limpiar, limpio**
clear—**claro**

clearly—claramente
clerk—dependiente, m
climb—subir
clock—reloj, m
close—cerrar (I)
clothes—ropa, f; vestidos, m
cloud—nube, f
coat—saco, m; americana, f
cobbler—zapatero, m
coffee—café, m
cold—frío (adj.); frío, m; resfriado, m
collect—cobrar
collide—chocar
collision—choque, m
colony—colonia, f
color—color, m
come—venir
commit—cometer
communist—comunista
companion—compañero, m
company—compañía, f
compartment—compartimiento, m
complete—completar, acabar, terminar,
   completo (adj.)
comply—cumplir
concerning—tocante (a), respecto (a),
   acerca de, en cuanto (a)
condemn—condenar
conduct—conducir
confess—confesar (I)
consent—consentir (II)
constable—alguacil, m
construct—construir
consul—cónsul, m
contain—contener
contain (be contained in)—caber
contented—contento
contents—contenidos, m
contract—contrato, m
contractor—contratista, m
converse—conversar
convict—condenar, convicto, m
cook—cocinar, cocinero, m
cool—fresco
cop—chote, m; jura, m
copper—cobre, m
corn—maíz, m
corner (inside)—rincón, m
corner (outside)—esquina, f
cornfield—milpa, f
corral—corral, m

correct—correcto, corregir (III)
cost—costar (I)
cotton—algodón, m
cotton (chop)—desahijar, limpiar
cotton (pick)—piscar
cotton picking—pisca, f
counsel—consejo, m; aconsejar
count—contar (I)
country (outside city)—campo, m
country (nation)—país, m
country (fatherland)—patria, f
countryman—campesino, m
countryman (fellow)—paisano, m
county—condado, m
court—corte, f; tribunal, m; juzgado, m
cousin—primo(a)
cover—cubrir
covered—cubierto
coveralls—overoles, m
cow—vaca, f
cowboy—vaquero, m
crawl—arrastrarse
crawl—andar a cuatro patas, (cat-like)
   gatear
crazy—loco
credit (on)—al fiado, crédito, m
creek—arroyo, m; riachuelo, m
crime—crimen, m; delito, m
crime (minor)—infracción de la ley
criminal—criminal, m; reo, m
crippled—cojo
cross—cruzar; cruz, f
cry—llorar, gritar, grito, m
cultivate—cultivar
cup—taza, f
customhouse—aduana, f
custom inspector—aduanero, m; inspector de aduana
cut—cortar; cortada, f

dad—papá, m
daily—diario
dairy—lechería, f
dam—presa, f
damage—daño, m; dañar
dance—bailar; baile, m
danger—peligro, m
dark—obscuro, moreno, prieto, trigueño
dark (become)—obscurecerse
date—fechar, fecha, f; cita, f; compromiso, m

daughter—hija, f
daughter-in-law—nuera, f
dawn—amanecer, m; madrugada, f
dawn—(verb), amanecer
day—día, m
day before yesterday—anteayer
day of rest—día de descanso
day after tomorrow—pasado mañana
dead—muerto (p. p. of morir)
deaf—sordo
dear (affection)—querido
dear (costly)—caro
death—muerte, f
debt—deuda, f
deceive—engañar
December—diciembre, m
decide—decidir
declare—declarar
deed—hecho, m; acto, m
deep—hondo
defendant—acusado, m
defect—defecto, m
delicious—delicioso
deliver—entregar
demand—demandar, demanda, f
dentist—dentista, m
deny—negar (I)
depart—salir, partir
departure—salida, f; partida, f
depend—depender
dependent—dependiente, m
deport—deportar
deportation—deportación, f
deported—deportado
describe—describir
description—descripción, f
desert—desierto, m
desire—desear, deseo, m
destination—destinación, f
detail—detalle, m
detain—detener
detective—detectivo, m; detective, m
die—morir (II)
difference—diferencia, f
different—diferente
difficult—difícil
dine—comer
dinner—comida, f
director—director, m
dirt—polvo, m; tierra, f
dirty—sucio, cochino°

dismiss—despedir (III)
dismiss (fire)—desocupar, despedir (III)
dispute—disgusto, m; mitote, m
distance—distancia, f
distant—distante
district—distrito, m; barrio, m
ditch—zanja, f; diche, m; canal, m; acequia, f
divide—dividir
divisional—divisorio
divorce—divorciar; divorcio, m
do—hacer
doctor—médico, m; doctor, m
document—documento, m
dog—perro, m
dollar—dólar, m; peso, m
domestic—doméstico
donkey—asno, m; burro, m
door—puerta, f
double—doble; doblar
doubt—dudar; duda, f
down—abajo, bajo
down (get)—bajarse de, apearse de
dozen—docena, f
dress—vestido, m; vestirse (III)
dress—traje, m
dressmaker—modista, f
drink—beber, tomar, trago, m
drive—manejar, guiar
driver—chofer, m; chófer, m
driver's license—licencia para manejar
drug—droga, f
druggist—droguero, m; boticario
drug store—botica, f; farmacia, f; droguería, f
drunk—borracho, ebrio, tomado
drunk (to become)—emborracharse
drunkard—borrachón, m
drunkenness—borracher(í)a, f
dry—secar, seco, árido
dump—dumpe, m
during—durante
dust—polvo, m
duty—deber, m; obligación, f
duties (custom)—derechos

each—cado, todo
eagle—el águila, f
ear (inner)—oído, m
ear (outer)—oreja, f
early—temprano

170

earn—ganar
earth—tierra, f
east—este, m; oriente, m
easy—fácil
easily—fácilmente
eat—comer
eat supper—cenar
eat breakfast—desayunarse
education—educación, f
Edward—Eduardo
egg—blanquillo, m; huevo, m
eight—ocho
eighteen—diez y ocho
eighth—octavo
eighty—ochenta
either—o
either . . . uno u otro
elbow—codo, m
electric—eléctrico
electricity—electricidad, f
elegant—elegante
elephant—elefante, m
eleven—once
embark—embarcar
emigrant—emigrante, m
employ—emplear; dar empleo, ocupar
employed—empleado
employee—empleado, m
employer—patrón, m; mayordomo, m
employment—empleo, m
empty—vacío
end—acabar; terminar
engine—locomotora, f; máquina, f
engineer—ingeniero, m; maquinista, m
English—inglés, m
English (adj.)—inglés(a)
enough—bastante, suficiente
enter—entrar, pasar°
entire—entero
entrance—entrada, f
entrance gate—garita, f
entry—entrada, f
envelope—sobre, m
equal—igual
errand—mandado, m; recado, m
error—error, m; falta, f
escape—escaparse, evadir
especial—especial
Europe—Europa
even—llano, liso
evening—tarde, f

ever—jamás, alguna vez, siempre
every—cada, todos
everybody—todo el mundo
everything—todo, todo lo que
everywhere—por todas partes
evidence—evidencia, f
exact—exacto, mero
exactly—exactamente, mero
examination—examen, m
examine—examinar, revisar, inspeccionar, registrar
example—ejemplo, m
excellent—excelente
exclude—excluir, negar la entrada
exclusion—exclusión, f
excuse—dispensar, excusar, excusa, f
exercise—ejercicio, m
explain—explicar
expect—esperar
expense—gasto, m; coste, m
export—exportar
express—expresar, manifestar (I); expreso, m; exprés, m
extend—extender (I)
extension—extensión, f
extra—extra
eye—ojo, m
eyebrow—ceja, f
eyeglasses—lentes, m; anteojos, m
eyelash—pestaña, f

fact—hecho, m
face—cara, f
fair—claro
faith—fe, f
fall—caer
false—falso
falsehood—falsedad, f
family—familia, f
far (away)—lejos
far from—lejos de
fare—pasaje, m
farm—hacienda, f; rancho, m
farmer—hacendado, m; agricultor, m
farm laborer—labrador, m; cultivador, m; sembrador, m
farther—más lejos
fast—recio, aprisa, rápido
fat—gordo, grueso
father—padre, m
father-in-law—suegro, m; papá, m

fault—**falta, m; culpa, f**
fear—**temer, tener miedo, miedo, m; temor, m**
February—**febrero, m**
federal—**federal**
fee—**derecho, m**
feel—**sentir(se) (III), tocar**
female—**hembra**
fence—**cerca, f**
few—**pocos**
fewer—**menos**
field—**labor, f; campo, m; sembrado, m**
fifteen—**quince**
fifth—**quinto**
fifty—**cincuenta**
fight—**pelear, combatir, pelea, f; combate, m**
file—**archivo, m; archivar**
file charges—**poner una queja**
fill—**llenar**
film—**película, f**
final—**final**
finally—**finalmente, al fin**
find—**hallar, encontrar (I)**
find out—**saber, averiguar**
fine—**imponer una multa; multar; multa, f**
fine—**bueno, fino**
finger—**dedo, m**
finish—**acabar, terminar, fin, m**
fire—**fuego, m; lumbre, m**
fire (a gun)—**tirar, disparar**
fire (dismiss)—**desocupar**
fireman—**bombero, m; fogonero, m**
first—**primero**
fish—**pez, m; pescado, m; pescar**
fisherman—**pescador, m**
five—**cinco**
five hundred—**quinientos**
fix—**arreglar, componer**
flag—**bandera, f**
flat—**punchada, f; flat, m; pinchada, f**
floor—**suelo, m; piso, m**
flour—**harina, f**
flower—**flor, f**
fly—**mosca, f**
fly—**volar (I)**
flood—**diluvio, m; inundación, f**
food—**comida, f**
fool—**tonto(a)**
foot—**pie, m; pata, f (animal)**

foot bridge—**tabla, f; puente de a pie**
foot path—**senda (de pie)**
forehead—**frente, f**
foreman—**mayordomo, m; patrón, m**
foreigner—**extranjero(a)**
forest—**selva, f; bosque, m**
forgery—**falsificación, f**
forget—**olvidar**
fork—**tenedor, m; horca, f**
former—**anterior**
former—**aquel**
forty—**cuarenta**
forward—**adelante, delante**
four—**cuatro**
fourth—**cuarto**
fourteen—**catorce**
Frank—**Francisco; Pancho**
free—**libre, libertar**
French—**francés (noun or adj.)**
frequently—**frecuentemente, a menudo**
fresh—**fresco**
friar—**fraile, m**
Friday—**viernes, m**
friend—**amigo(a)**
friend (close)—**compadre, m**
from—**de, desde**
front—**delantero, frente**
front of—**delante de**
fruit—**fruta, f**
full—**lleno**
fulfill—**cumplir**
furniture—**muebles, m**
furniture store—**mueblería, f**
future—**futuro, m; porvenir, m**

gain—**ganar**
gallon—**galón, m**
garage—**garage, m; garaje, m**
garden—**jardín, m**
gardener—**jardinero, m**
garments—**ropa, f; vestidos, m; prendas de vestir**
gas—**gas, m**
gasoline—**gasolina, f**
gate—**puerta, f; entrada, f**
gate (entrance)—**garita, f**
gather—**piscar, coger**
gentleman—**caballero, m; señor, m**
generally—**generalmente**
George—**Jorge**
German—**alemán, m; alemán (adj.)**

Germany—Alemania
get—obtener, conseguir (III), sacar
get (into vehicle)—subir(se) a
get (out or off of a vehicle)—bajar(se)
de
get up—levantarse
gift—regalo, m
girl—muchacha, f; niña, f
give—dar
glance—mirada, f; ojeada, f
glass (drinking)—vaso
glass—vidrio, m
glove—guante, m
go—ir
to go away—irse
goat—chivo, m; cabra, f
goatherd—chivero, m; pastor, m;
borreguero, m; cabrero, m
God—Dios
goddaughter—ahijada, f
godfather—padrino, m
godmother—madrina, f
godson—ahijado, m
gold—oro, m
good—bueno
good afternoon—buenas tardes
good-bye—adiós, hasta luego, hasta la
vista
good morning—buenos días
good night—buenas noches
government—gobierno, m
granddaughter—nieta, f
grandfather—abuelo, m
grandmother—abuela, f
grandson—nieto, m
grasp—agarrar
grass—yerba, f; sacate, m
grass—pasto, m; hierba, f
grave yard—panteón, m; cementerio, m
gray—gris
great—grande, famoso
green—verde
greet—saludar
grey—gris
grocer—abacero, m
groceries—abarrotes, m
ground—suelo, m; tierra, f
grow (plants)—cultivar
grow—crecer
grow (dark)—anochecer, obscurecerse
guard—guardar, guardia, f, m

guide—guiar, guía, f, m
guilty—culpable
gulch—cañada, f; quebrada, f
gulf—golfo, m
gun—fusil, m; (shotgun—escopeta, f)
gun shot—tiro, m; disparo, m; balazo,
m

hair—pelo, m; cabello, m
hairy—peludo, velludo
half—medio, mitad, f (noun)
half-brother—medio hermano
half-sister—media hermana
halt—alto, hacer alto, parar
ham—jamón, m
hand—mano, f
hand (verb)—entregar
handcuffs—esposas, f; manilla, f
hang up—colgar (I)
history—historia, f
happen—suceder, pasar, ocurrir
happy—feliz, alegre, contento
hard—duro
hard (difficult)—difícil
hard (a great deal)—mucho
harm—dañar, daño, m
harvest—cosecha, f; cosechar
hat—sombrero, m
hate—odiar, odio, m
have—tener
have—(auxiliary) haber
hay—heno, m; sacate, m
he—él
head—cabeza, f
headtax—capitación, f
health—salud, f
healthy—de buena salud
hear—oír, oír decir
hearing (by jury)—juicio por jurado
hearing—audiencia, f
heart—corazón, m
to heat—calentar (I)
heat—calor, m
heater—calorífero, m
heavy—pesado, grueso
height—altura, f; estatura, f
Helen—Elena
hell—infierno, m
hello—¿qué húbole? ¡oiga!, hola
help—ayudar, ayuda, f; asistir
hen—gallina, f

Henry—Enrique

her—(direct object) la, (indirect object) le, (preposition) ella, (possessive) de ella, su

hers—el suyo, la suya, los suyos, las suyas

here—aquí, acá

hide—piel, f; cuero, m; esconder, ocultar

hidden—escondido

high—alto

high priced—caro, costoso

highway—carretera, f

hill—sierra, f; loma, f; cerro, m; colina, f

him—(direct object) le, lo

hire—ocupar, dar empleo

his—(possessive adjective) su

his—(possessive pronoun) el suyo, la suya, los suyos, las suyas

hit—golpear, pegar

hog—puerco, m; marrano, m; cerdo, m; cochino, m

hole (as in wall)—abertura, f

hole (as in fence)—hoyo, m

hole (as in ground)—pozo, m; hueco, m

holiday—día de fiesta

home—hogar, m; casa, f

home (at)—en casa

hope—esperar, esperanza, f

horn (auto)—bocina, f; pito, m

horn (animal)—cuerno, m

horse—caballo, m

hose—medias, f

hose (garden)—manguera, f

hospital—hospital, m

hot—caliente, caluroso

hotel—hotel, m

hour—hora, f

house—casa, f; hogar, m; domicilio, m

household goods—menaje de casa, m; muebles, m

housekeeper—ama de llaves, doméstica, f

housewife—ama de casa

how?—¿cómo?

however—sin embargo

how many?—¿cuántos(as)?

how much?—¿cuánto(a)?

hundred—ciento (cien)

hunger—hambre, f

hungry (to be)—tener hambre

hunt for—buscar

hunt—cazar

hurry—darse prisa, apresurarse, ¡ándale!

hurt—doler (I); lastimar; herir (II)

husband—esposo, m; marido, m

I—yo

ice—hielo, m

ice cream—helado, m; nieve, f

idea—idea, f

identification—identificación, f

identify—identificar

idiot—idiota, m, f

if—si

ill—enfermo, malo

illegitimate—ilegítimo

illegitimate child—hijo natural

illegal—ilegal

illness—enfermedad, f

immediately—inmediatamente

immediately—enseguida

immigrant—inmigrante, m

immigrant inspector—inspector de inmigración

immigrate—inmigrar

immigration—inmigración, f

immoral—inmoral

import—importar

importance—importancia, f

important—importante

impossible—imposible

imprison—encarcelar, poner preso

in—en

inch—pulgada, f

independence—independencia, f

independent—independiente

Indian—indio (noun or adj.)

indolence—desidia, f; indolencia, f

industry—industria, f

in front of—delante de

inhabitant—habitante, m

ink—tinta, f

innocent—inocente

insane—loco

inside—dentro

inspector—inspector, m

inspect—inspeccionar, examinar

instead of—en vez de, en lugar de

intend—pensar (I), tener la intención, intentar (I)
intention—intención, f
intimate—íntimo
interest—interés, m
interior—interior, m
interpret—interpretar
investigate—investigar
investigation—investigación, f
invite—invitar, convidar
iron—hierro, m; fierro, m
iron (clothes)—planchar, plancha, f
island—isla, f
it—lo, la
Italian—italiano, m; (adj.) italiano(a)
Italy—Italia
its—su

jacket—chaqueta, f
jail, cárcel, f; bote, m (can)
James—Jaime
Jane—Juana
janitor—portero, m; conserje, m
January—enero, m
jeweler—joyero, m
jaw—quijada, f; mandíbula, f
Joe—José, Pepe
John—Juan
join—juntar, unir
Josephine—Josefina
judge—juzgar, juez, m
July—julio, m
juice—jugo, m
jump—brincar, saltar
June—junio, m
jury—jurado, m
justice of peace—juez de paz

keep—guardar
key—llave, f
khaki—kaki, m; caqui, m
kill—matar
kind—clase, f; tipo, m; bondadoso
kitchen—cocina, f
kitchen utensils—batería (trastos) de cocina
knee—rodilla, f
knife—navaja, f; cuchillo, m
knife (large)—machete, m
knife—(pen) cortaplumas, m
know—saber

know (be acquainted with)—conocer

labor—labor, f; trabajo, m; trabajar
laborer—trabajador, m; jornalero, m
lack—faltar; falta, f
lady—dama, señora, f
lake—lago, m; laguna, f
lamb—cordero, m
lame—cojo
land—tierra, f; terreno, m
landlord—patrón, m
language—idioma, m; lengua, f
large—grande
large (very)—grandote
larger—más grande
largest—el or la más grande
lasso—lazo, m
last—durar
last—último, pasado
last night—anoche
late—tarde
later—más tarde, después
lately—últimamente, recientemente
latter—éste(a)
laundry—lavandería, f
law—ley, f
lawyer—abogado, m; licenciado, m
laziness—desidia, f; pereza, f
lazy—perezoso, flojo
leaf—hoja, f
lead—plomo, m
lean—flaco
learn—aprender
least—el or la menor
least (at)—a lo menos, por lo menos
leather—cuero, m
leave—salir, partir, dejar
left—izquierdo
leg—pierna, f
legal—legal
legally—legalmente
lemon—limón, m
lend—prestar
length—largo, m; longitud, m
less—menos
lesson—lección, f
let—dejar, permitir
level—plano, llano, nivel
liberate—libertar, librar
liberty—libertad, f
license—licencia, f

175

license plates—placas, f
lie—mentir (II); mentira, f
lie—decir (echar) mentiras
lie down—acostarse (I); tenderse (I)
life—vida, f
lift—levantar, alzar
light (weight)—ligero
   (color)—claro
light—luz, f; luminar
light (verb)—encender (I); prender;
  (electric)—luz eléctrica; (globe)—
  foco, m
like—semejante
like—como, lo mismo que
like (verb)—gustar
limit—límite, m
line—línea, f; raya, f
lip—labio, m
list—lista, f
little—poco
listen—escuchar
little (size)—pequeño, chico, chiquito
little (quantity)—poco
live—vivir
living—vida, f; subsistencia, f
load—carga, f; cargar
local—local
long—largo
longer (time)—más tiempo
look at—mirar
look for—buscar
loose—suelto
loosen—aflojar, soltar (I)
lose—perder (I)
Louis—Luis
Louise—Luisa
love—amar, querer a (I)
low—bajo, abajo
lower—bajar
lower—más bajo, más abajo
luck—suerte, f
lunch—lonche, m; merienda, f
lunch counter—lonchería, f
lungs—pulmones, m

mad—enojado
maid—criada, f
mail—correo, m
maintain—mantener, sostener
make—hacer
mamma—mamá, f

man—hombre, m
manager—gerente, m; director, m
manner—manera, f; modo, m
many—muchos(as)
map—mapa, m
March—marzo, m
march—marchar
mare—yegua, f
mark—marcar, marca, f
market—mercado, m
marriage—casamiento, m; matrimonio
marriage certificate—certificado de matrimonio
marry—casarse con
Martha—Marta
Mary—María
mason—albañil, m
match—fósforo, m; mecha, f
match—cerilla, f
matter—asunto, m; negocio, m
May—mayo, m
may—poder (I) (to be able)
maybe—tal vez, quizás
mayor—alcalde, m
mayor—presidente municipal
meal—comida, f
mean—querer (I) decir
meanwhile—mientras tanto
meat—carne, f
meat market—canicería, f
mechanic—mecánico, m
medicine—medicina, f
meet—encontrar (I)
meet (become acquainted)—conocer
meeting—mitin, m; junta, f
member—miembro, m
menu—lista, f
merchant—comerciante, m
metal—metal, m
Mexican—mexicano(a)
Mexico—México, Méjico
middle—medio
midnight—medianoche, f
midwife—partera, f
mile—milla, f
milk—leche, f
mill—molina, f
miller—molinero, m
mine (possessive pronoun)—el mío, la
  mía, los míos, las mías
mine—mina, f

176

miner—minero, m
mineral—mineral, m
minor—menor (de edad)
minus—menos
minute—minuto, m
Miss—señorita, f; Srta.
mistake—falta, f; error, m
mole—lunar, m
moment—momento, m
Monday—lunes, m
money—dinero, m
month—mes, m
moon—luna, f
more—más
morning—mañana, f
mother—madre, f
mother-in-law—suegra, f
motor—motor, m
mount—montar; montura
mountain—montaña, f
mouth—boca, f
move—mover (I)
movie—cine, m
Mr.—señor, Sr.
Mrs.—señora, Sra.
much—mucho
mud—lodo
mule—mula, f
murder—asesinar
murderer—asesinato, m
music—música, f
musician—músico, m
mustache—bigote, m
my—mi

name—nombre, m
named (to be)—llamarse
narrow—angosto, estrecho
nation—nación, f
nationality—nacionalidad, f
native—nativo(a)
naturalize—naturalizar
naturalization—naturalización, f
necessary—necesario
neck—cuello, m; pescuezo, m—(Mexican, also of animal)
need—necesitar, faltar
neighbor—vecino(a)
neither—ni, tampoco
neither . . . nor—ni . . . ni
nephew—sobrino, m

never—nunca, jamás
nevertheless—sin embargo
new—nuevo
newspaper—periódico, m; diario, m
next—próximo, que viene, siguiente
nickname—apodo, m
niece—sobrina, f
night—noche, f
nightfall—anochecer, m
nine—nueve
nineteen—diez y nueve
ninety—noventa
ninth—noveno
no—no
nobody—nadie
noise—ruido, m
none—ninguno(a)
noon—mediodía, m
nor—ni
north—norte, m
North American—norteamericano(a)
nose—nariz, f
not—no
nothing—nada
November—noviembre, m
now—ahora
nowadays—hoy día
right now—ahorita
number—número, m
nurse—nodriza, f; enfermera, f
nurse (for children)—niñera, f
nut—nuez, f

oak—roble, m
oath—juramento, m
oath—(to take) prestar juramento; tomar juramento; declarar bajo juramento
observe—observar
obtain—obtener
occupation—ocupación, f; oficio, m
occupied—ocupado
occupy—ocupar
occur—ocurrir, suceder
October—octubre, m
of—de
offense—ofensa, f
offer—ofrecer
offer—oferta, f
office—oficina, f; despacho, m
officer—oficial, m; dignatario, m

official—oficial, m
often—a menudo
oil—aceite, m
old—viejo
older—mayor
on—en, sobre, encima de
once—una vez
at once—en seguida
one—uno, una
only—único, sólo, solamente
open—abrir
opened—abierto
opportunity—oportunidad, f
or—o
orange—naranja, f
order—mandar
orphan—huérfano, m
other—otro
ought—deber
our—nuestro
ours—el nuestro, etc.
out—fuera, afuera
over—sobre, encima de
overalls—overoles, m
overcoat—abrigo, m; sobretodo, m
over yonder—allá
owe—deber
owner—dueño, m

package—paquete, m; bulto, m
page—página, f
pain—dolor, m; doler (I)
paint—pintar, pinto, m
painter—pintor, m
pair—par, m
paper—papel, m
papa—papá, m
pardon—perdonar, perdón, m
parents—padres, m
park—parque, m; estacionarse
part—parte, f; partir
pass—pasar, paso, m
passage—pasaje, m
passenger—pasajero, m
passport—pasaporte, m
past—pasado, último
pasture—pasto, m; pastura, f
path—sendero, m; vereda, f
Paul—Pablo
paved—pavimentado
paw—pata, f

pay—pagar
pay day—día de pagos
peach—durazno, m; melocotón, m
pear—pera, f
pen (writing)—pluma, f
pen (stock)—corral, m
pencil—lápiz, m
penitentiary—penitenciario, m; pinta, f;
    presidio, m
penny—centavo, m
people—gente, f; pueblo, m
perhaps—tal vez, quizás, puede ser
perjury—perjurio, m
permanently—permanentement
permission—permiso, m; permisión, f
permit—permitir, permiso, m
person—persona, f
photograph—fotografía, f; retrato, m
pick (cotton)—piscar
pick (choose)—escoger
pick up—levantar, coger
picture (person)—retrato, m
        (on wall)—cuadro, m
        (engraved)—grabado, m
        (painting)—pintura, f
picture show—cine, m
picture film—película, f
piece—pedazo, m; pieza, f
pimple—granujo, m; espinilla, f
pin—alfiler, m; broche, m
pistol—pistola, f
pits (small pox)—viruelas, f
pitted—pitada
place—lugar, m; sitio, m
place—colocar, poner
plant—plantar, planta, f; sembrar (I)
planter—sembrador, m; plantador, m
play—jugar (I), juego, m
plaza—plaza, f
please—gustar, agradar
please—por favor
plow—arar, arado, m
plumber—plomero, m
pocket—bolsillo, m
pocket-book—bolsa, f; portamonedas, m
point—punto, m
pole—palo, m
police force—la policía
police officer—el policía
poor—pobre
poor (lean)—flaco

poplar—álamo, m (cottonwood)
popular—popular
port—puerto, m
porter—cargador, m; portero, m
portrait—retrato, m
possible—posible
post—poste, m; palo, m
postmaster—administrador (jefe) de correos, m
post office—correo, m; estafeta, f
potato (Irish)—papa, f; patata, f
potato (sweet)—camote, m; batata, f
pound—libra, f
power—poder, m; fuerza, f
preceding—anterior
prefer—preferir (II)
prepare—preparar
present—presente
present (gift)—regalo
present—presentar
president—presidente, m
pretty—bonito, lindo
price—precio, m
priest—cura, m; sacredote, m
prison—prisión, m; cárcel, f; juzgado, m
proceedings—actas, f; autos, m; procedimientos, m
prohibit—prohibir
promise—prometer, promesa, f
promoter—promotor, m; empresario, m
proof—prueba, f; comprobantes, m; constancia, f
property—propiedad, f
prove—probar (I), comprobar (I)
punish—castigar
pupil—alumno(a); estudiante, m or f; discípulo(a)
purchase—comprar, compra, f
pure—puro
purse—bolsa, f; portamonedas, m
push—empujar
put—poner, colocar
put on—ponerse

quarrel—barulla, f; disgusto, m
quart—cuarto, m
quarter—cuarto, m
question—pregunta, f; cuestión, f
quick—pronto
quickly—pronto

rabbit—conejo, m; liebre, f
race—raza, f
radio—radio, f
rag—trapo, m
railroad—ferrocarril, m
railroad track—rieles, m; traque, m
raise—criar
rain—llover (I), lluvia, f
Ralph—Rafael, Raúl
ranch—rancho, m
rancher—ranchero, m
ranch foreman—caporal, m
rat—rata, f
ravine—arroyo, m; cañada, f
raw—crudo
read—leer
read—listo
reap—cosechar
reason—razón, f; causa, f
receipt—recibo, m
receive—recibir
recently—recientemente
record—record, m; constancia, f; registrar, apuntar
red—colorado, rojo
reenlisted—reenganchado
relative—pariente, m
relax—aflojar, soltar (I)
release—libertar, poner en libertad
remain—permanecer, durar, quedarse, estarse
remember—recordar (I), acordarse (I)
renew—renovar (I)
rent—rentar, alquilar, arrendar (I)
rent—renta, f
repair—reparar, componer
repair—reparo, m
repeat—repetir (III)
report—informe, m; reporte, m; reportar, informar
republic—república, f
requirement—requisito, m
reside—residir, morar, vivir
residence—residencia, f; domicilio, m; casa, f; morada, f
resources—los bienes; riquezas, f
retail—al por menor
return—regresar, volver (I), regreso, m; vuelta, f
return (object)—devolver (I)

reveal—revelar, mostrar (I), demostrar (I)

revolver—revólver, m

rich—rico

Richard—Ricardo

ride (auto, train)—viajar en auto (tren)

rifle—rifle, m

right—derecho, m; razón, f

rights—derechos

ring—anillo, m; sortija, f

river—río, m

road—camino, m

roast—asar

rob—robar

robber—ladrón, m

robbery—robo, m

Robert—Roberto

rock—piedra, f

roof—techo, m

room—cuarto, m; pieza, f

rope—reata, f; lazo, m; mecate, m; soga, f; cuerda, f

rough—áspero

round—redondo

route—rumbo, m; ruta, f

rule—regla, f

run—correr

sad—triste

safe—salvo, seguro

sailor—marinero, m

salary—sueldo, m, salario, m

sale—venta, f

saloon—cantina, f; salón, m

salt—sal, f

same—mismo, igual

sand—arena, f

sandwich—sandwich, m; emparedado, m

satisfied—contento; satisfecho; conforme

Saturday—sábado, m

say—decir

scales—balanzas, f

scar—cicatriz, f; seña, f

scar (cut)—cortada, f

school—escuela, f

search—registrar

search for—buscar

season—estación, f

seat (oneself)—sentarse (I)

seat—asiento

seated—sentado

second—segundo

secretary—secretario, m

see—ver

seed—semilla, f

seek—buscar

seem—parecer

sell—vender

send—mandar, enviar, expedir (III)

sentence—condenar, sentenciar, condena, f; fallo, m; sentencia, f

sentence—frase, f; oración, f

separate—separar

September—septiembre, m

servant—criado(a); doméstico(a); mozo(a)

serve (sentence)—cumplir una condena

set—poner, colocar

seven—siete

seventeen—diez y siete

seventh—séptimo

seventy—setenta

several—varios(as), algunos(as)

sex—sexo

sharecropper—mediero, m

shave—afeitar(se); rasurar

she—ella

shear (sheep)—trasquilar

sheep—borrego(a), oveja, f

sheriff—sherife, m; jerife, m

ship—buque, m; vapor, m; barco, m

shirt—camisa, f

shoe—zapato, m

shoe store—zapatería, f

shoot—tirar, disparar, fusilar

shop—tienda, f; taller, m

shore—orilla, f

short—corto, bajo

short (man)—chapo, m

shot—bala, m; balazo, m; disparo, m

shoulder—hombro, m

show—enseñar, mostrar (I)

shut—cerrar (I)

sick—enfermo, malo

side—lado, m

sidewalk—acera, f; banqueta, f

sight—vista, f

sign—firmar; signo, m; señal, f; seña, f

signature—firma, f

silk—seda, f

silver—plata, f

since—desde, pues
sing—cantar
single—solo
single (person)—soltero(a)
sir—señor
sister—hermana, f
sister-in-law—cuñada, f
sit down—sentarse (I)
site—sitio, m; lugar, m
six—seis
sixteen—diez y seis
sixth—sexto
sixty—sesenta
size—tamaño, m
skin—piel, f; cutis, f
skinny—flaco
sky—cielo, m
sleep—dormir (II), sueño, m
slim—delgado; flaco
slipper—zapatilla, f
slow—despacio, lento
slowly—lentamente, despacio
small—pequeño, chico
smoke—fumar, humo, m
smooth—suave, liso, llano
smuggle—pasar de contrabando
smuggler—contrabandista, m
snake—víbora, f; culebra, f
rattlesnake—víbora de cascabel
sneeze—estornudar
snow—nevar (I); nieve, f
so—así, tan
soap—jabón, m
sock—calcetín, m
so much—tanto(a)
so many—tantos(as)
soft—suave, blando
soil—tierra, f; suelo, m
soldier—soldado, m
solicit—solicitar
some—alguno
somebody—alguien, alguna persona
something—algo, alguna cosa
son—hijo, m
son-in-law—yerno, m
soon—pronto
sort—clase, f; modo, m
soup—caldo, m; sopa, f
south—sur, m; sud
sow—sembrar (I)
Spain—España

Spaniard—español(a)
Spanish—español, m; (adj.) español(a)
speak—hablar
special—especial
spectacles—anteojos, m; (eye glasses) lentes, m
speed—velocidad, f
spend (money)—gastar
    (time)—pasar
spoon—cuchara, f
spoon (tea)—cucharilla, f; cucharita, f
spot—mancha, f
spot (place)—sitio, m; lugar, m
spotted—manchado
spring—primavera, f
square—plaza, f
square—cuadrado
stage (coach)—diligencia, f; esteche, m
stairs—escaleras, f
stamp—timbre, m; sello, m; estampilla, f; estampar
star—estrella, f
start—empezar (I), comenzar (I), principiar, ponerse en marcha
state—estado, m; declarar
statement—declaración, f
station—estación, f
stay—quedarse, permanecer
steal—robar
steamer trunk—petaca, f
steer—novillo, m
step-daughter—hijastra, f; entenada, f
step—paso, m
steps (stairs)—escaleras, f
stepfather—padrastro, m
stepmother—madrastra, f
stepson—hijastro, m; entenado, m
stick—palo, m; bastón, m
still—todavía, tranquilo
stomach—estómago, m
stone—piedra, f
stop—alto
store—tienda, f
story (floor)—piso, m
story—cuento, m; historia, f
stove—estufa, f
stowaway—polizón, m
straight—derecho, recto, directo
stranger—extranjero, m; desconocido, m
straw—paja, f
street—calle, f

street car—**tranvía, m**
strength—**fuerza, f; vigor, m**
strike of men—**huelga, f**
strike—**pegar, golpear, golpe, f**
striped—**listado, rayado**
strong—**fuerte**
student—**alumno(a), estudiante**
study—**estudiar, estudio, m**
suburb—**barrio, m; colonia, f**
suddenly—**de repente**
sue—**poner una queja, poner pleito**
suffer—**sufrir, padecer**
sugar—**azúcar, m**
suit—**traje, m; vestido, m**
suit (law)—**pleito, m; queja, f**
suitcase—**maleta, f**
sum—**suma, f**
summer—**verano, m**
sun—**sol, m**
Sunday—**domingo, m**
supper—**cena, f**
sure—**seguro, cierto**
surname—**apellido, m**
swear—**jurar, hacer juramento**
swim—**nadar**
sweet—**dulce**

table—**mesa, f**
tail—**cola, f; rabo, m**
tailor—**sastre, m**
tailor shop—**sastrería, f**
take—**tomar, llevar, aceptar**
take away—**quitar**
take off—**quitarse**
take out—**sacar**
take steps to—**hacer arreglos**
talk—**hablar**
tall—**alto**
tank—**tanque, m**
tattoo—**tatú, m; tatuaje, m; grabado, m; pintura, f**
taxi—**taxi, m; carro de sitio, m**
tea—**té, m**
teach—**enseñar**
teacher—**maestro, m; profesor, m**
teeth—**dientes, m**
telegram—**telegrama, m**
telephone—**teléfono, m; telefonear**
tell—**decir**
ten—**diez**
tend—**cuidar**

tenth—**décimo**
tequila—**tequila, m**
testimony—**testimonio, m; declaración, f**
thank—**dar gracias**
thanks—**gracias, f**
that—(relative) **que**, (demonstrative) **aquel, ese**
theater—**teatro, m**
the—**el, m; la, f; los, m; las, f**
their—**su, sus**
theirs—**el suyo, etc.**
them—(direct object) **los, las** (prepositional pronoun) **ellos, ellas**
then—**entonces, luego, después**
there—**allá, allí, ahí**
these—**estos(as)**
they—**ellos, ellas**
thick—**grueso, espeso, denso**
thief—**ladrón, m**
thin—**delgado, fino, flaco**
thing—**cosa**
think—**pensar (I), creer**
third—**tercero**
thirteen—**trece**
thirty—**treinta**
this—**este, esta**
Thomas—**Tomás**
those—**esos, esas, aquellos(as)**
thousand—**mil**
three—**tres**
through—**por**
throw—**tirar, echar, lanzar**
Thursday—**jueves, m**
thus—**así, de este modo**
ticket—**boleto, m; billete, m; tiquete, m**
time—**tiempo (period), m; vez (numerical), f; hora (time of day), f**
tin—**estaño, m; lata, f; hojalata, f**
tire—**llanta, f; neumático, m**
tire—**cansar**
tired—**cansado**
to—**a, hasta**
tobacco—**tabaco, m**
today—**hoy**
toe—**dedo (del pie), m**
together—**juntos, junto con**
toilet—**excusado, m; retrete, m**
tomato—**tomate, m**
tomorrow—**mañana, f**
tonight—**esta noche, f**
tongue—**lengua, f**

too—también, además
too many—demasiados(as)
too much—demasiado, (adj.) demasiado
tools—herramientas, f
top—cima, f; cumbre, f
top (beets)—descoronar, topear
tourist—turista, m
town—pueblo, m; población, f
track—huella, f; seguir la pista
track (railroad)—traque, m; rieles
trail—sendero, m; vereda, f
train—tren, m
travel—viajar, caminar
traveler—viajero(a)
tree—árbol, m
trial—juzgado, m; prueba, f
trip—viaje, m; excursión, f
trousers—pantalones, m
truck—camión, m; troca, m; troque, m
true—verdad, f; verdadero, sincero
trunk—baúl, m; petaca, f
truth—verdad, f
try—tratar de, procurar
try (trial)—juzgar
Tuesday—martes, m
turkey—guajalote, m; pavo, m; cócono, m
turn—doblar, dar vuelta a, volver (I)
twelve—doce
twenty—veinte
twin—cuate, m; gemelo, m
two—dos

ugly—feo
uncle—tío, m
under—bajo, abajo, debajo
The United States—Los Estados Unidos
until—hasta, hasta que
up—arriba
up (get)—levantarse
upon—sobre, en
upon oath—bajo juramento
upstairs—arriba
us (prep.)—nosotros(as)
us (obj.)—nos
use—usar

vaccination—vacuna, f
valid—válido
valley—valle, m
value—valor, m; precio, m

various—varios(as), diferentes
verb—verbo, m
verify—verificar
very—muy
vest—chaleco, m
view—vista, f
vinegar—vinagre, m
violate—violar, infringir
visa—visar, f; visar (verb)
visit—visitar, visita, f
visitor—visita, m or f; visitador, m; visitante, m
voice—voz, f
voluntary—voluntario
voluntary—voluntariamente
vote—votar; voto, m

wade—vadear, andar a pie por el agua
wages—sueldo, m
wagon—vagón, m; carreta, f
wait—esperar, aguardar
waiter—mozo(a), criado(a), mesero(a), camarero(a)
waive (law)—ceder, renunciar a
walk—andar
wall—pared, f; muralla, f
want—querer (I), desear, necesitar
war—guerra, f
warm—caliente, caluroso, calentar (III)
warn—avisar
warrant (of arrest)—fallo de arresto, orden de arresto
wart—verruga, f
wash—lavar(se)
washerwoman—lavandera, f
watch—reloj, m
watch—guardar, cuidar
watchmaker—relojero, m
water—el agua, f; regar (I)
we—nosotros(as)
weak—débil
wear—llevar, tener puesto
weather—tiempo, m
Wednesday—miércoles, m
weed—yerba, f
week—semana, f; ocho días
weigh—pesar, considerar
weight—peso, m
well—pozo, m; noria, f; pues, bien
west—oeste, m; poniente, m
wet—mojar, mojado

what?—¿qué?
whatever—cualquier(a)
wheel—rueda, f
when?—¿cuándo?
when—cuando
where?—¿dónde?
where—donde
whether—si
which?—¿cuál?
which (relative)—que
while—mientras
white—blanco
who?—¿quién?
who (relative)—que, quien
whole—entero, todo
wholesale—al por mayor, en grande
whom—a quien
whose—cuyo
whose?—¿de quién?
why?—¿por qué?
wide—ancho
widow—viuda, f
widower—viudo, m
width—anchura, f; ancho, m
William—Guillermo
win—ganar, vencer
windshield—parabrisa, m
wind—viento, m; aire, m; brisa, f
window—ventana, f; ventanilla
wine—vino, m
winter—invierno, m
wire—alambre, m
wise—sabio, docto, erudito
wish—querer (I), desear
with—con, en compañía de
within—dentro de
without—sin, fuera, afuera
witness—testigo, m
wolf—lobo, m or f

woman—mujer, f
wood—madera, f
wood (fire)—leña, f
wood chopper—leñador, m
woods—monte, m; bosque, m
wool—lana, f
word—palabra, f
work—trabajar, obrar, trabajo, m; empleo, m; obra, f
worker—trabajador, m; jornalero, m
workshop—taller, m
world—mundo, m
worry—apurarse, afligir
worse—peor
worst—el peor, la peor, etc.
wreck—choque, m; chocar
wrinkle—arruga, f
wrist—muñeca, f; pulsera, f
write—escribir

yard (house)—patio, m; yarda, f; corral, m
yard (measure)—yarda, f; vara, f
year—año, m
yell—gritar
yellow—amarillo
yes—sí
yesterday—ayer
yet—todavía
yonder—allá
you—usted, ustedes (polite)
you—tú, vosotros(as) (familiar)
young—joven
younger—menor
youngest—el menor, etc.
young lady—señorita, f
your—su
yours—el suyo, etc.

W